Jumbo Bank Statement Mortgage Loans

How to Finance High-Value Properties Using Bank Statement Income

By Joseph G. Correa

Licensed Mortgage Broker

Finibi Mortgage

Copyright & Legal Notice

Published by Live Stronger Faster

The information provided in this book is for educational and informational purposes only and does not constitute financial, legal, tax, or investment advice. Although the author is a licensed mortgage professional, the content presented is general in nature and is not intended as personalized guidance for any specific individual or financial situation.

The strategies, structuring methods, and examples discussed in this book are illustrative and educational in nature. They are intended to demonstrate concepts related to bank statement mortgage loan qualification and structuring, including deposit analysis, expense ratio application, and investor guideline interpretation. These examples do not represent guaranteed outcomes or approvals. Results may vary significantly based on individual financial profiles, documentation, credit history, property type, and lender-specific requirements.

The author and publisher make no representations or warranties regarding the accuracy, completeness, or applicability of the content and disclaim any liability for errors, omissions, or outcomes resulting from the use or misuse of the information contained in this book.

All trademarks, service marks, company names, and product names referenced in this publication are the property of their respective owners and are used strictly for identification and educational purposes only. Their inclusion does not imply endorsement or affiliation.

First Edition, 2026

Table of Contents

Introduction

In the world of mortgage financing, there is a clear dividing line between conventional lending and the flexible, opportunity-driven strategies that allow borrowers to step into higher price points, premium neighborhoods, and legacy-level real estate. That dividing line becomes even more apparent when we enter the realm of jumbo financing. Jumbo loans are not simply larger versions of conventional loans—they are a completely different category, governed by stricter guidelines, heightened risk assessments, and a deeper level of scrutiny. For self-employed borrowers, entrepreneurs, and high-income individuals who do not fit the traditional mold of tax-return-based underwriting, this world can feel out of reach. But the truth is, with the right structure, the right documentation, and the right strategy, jumbo bank statement mortgage loans open doors that many borrowers never realize are available to them.

This book exists to bridge that gap. It is designed to show you how to move beyond the limitations of conventional underwriting and step confidently into the world of high-value property financing using bank statement income. Whether you are purchasing a luxury primary residence, a high-end investment property, or refinancing into a better financial position, understanding how jumbo bank statement loans work can transform your financial trajectory. These loans are not reserved for the ultra-wealthy with perfect documentation—they are built for borrowers with strong financial profiles that simply do not fit inside traditional boxes.

The foundation of jumbo bank statement lending lies in understanding that income is not always best represented on tax returns. In fact, for many successful individuals, tax returns can significantly understate true earning power due to deductions, reinvestment strategies, and business structuring. This creates a disconnect between what a borrower earns and what a traditional lender sees. Jumbo bank statement loans solve this problem by shifting the focus away from tax returns and toward actual cash flow. By analyzing deposits over a defined period—typically twelve or twenty-four months—lenders can establish a more accurate representation of income, especially for business owners and self-employed professionals.

However, with greater opportunity comes greater responsibility. Jumbo loans carry higher loan amounts, which means lenders assume more risk. Because of this, guidelines are often more conservative, and the margin for error becomes smaller. This is where knowledge becomes your greatest advantage. Borrowers who understand how to properly present their financial profile, structure their accounts, and highlight compensating factors can position themselves for approvals that might otherwise seem impossible.

One of the key elements of success in jumbo bank statement lending is the concept of compensating factors. Unlike standard loans, where qualification can often feel like a checklist, jumbo loans require a more holistic evaluation. Lenders are not just asking, "Does this borrower meet the minimum requirements?" They are asking, "Does this borrower present a strong overall risk profile?" This means that strengths in one area can offset weaknesses in another. For example, a borrower with slightly lower credit may still qualify if they demonstrate strong reserves, significant liquidity, consistent deposits, or a low debt-to-income ratio. Understanding how to build and present these compensating factors is a critical skill that this book will help you develop.

Another important aspect of jumbo bank statement loans is the role of overlays. While standard mortgage products often follow widely accepted guidelines, jumbo loans are heavily influenced by lender-specific requirements. These overlays can vary significantly from one lender to another, affecting everything from maximum loan amounts and loan-to-value ratios to reserve requirements and acceptable income calculations. This variability can be frustrating for borrowers who are unfamiliar with the landscape, but it also creates opportunity. By understanding how different lenders interpret risk and structure their programs, you can position yourself to find the right fit for your unique financial profile.

As you progress through this book, you will begin to see that jumbo bank statement lending is not just about qualifying for a loan—it is about engineering an approval. This means taking a proactive approach to your finances, identifying potential red flags before they become obstacles, and structuring your documentation in a way that tells a clear, compelling story. Every deposit, every account, and every financial decision plays a role in how your file is perceived. When done correctly, your financial profile becomes more than just a set of numbers—it becomes a narrative of stability, growth, and reliability.

For many borrowers, the idea of purchasing a high-value property feels intimidating, not because they lack the financial capacity, but because they lack the clarity on how to navigate the process. Traditional lending systems were not designed with entrepreneurs, freelancers, and business owners in mind. They were built around predictable, salaried income. As a result, borrowers who fall outside of that structure often feel excluded, even when they are financially stronger than many who qualify through conventional means. Jumbo bank statement loans represent a shift toward a more realistic and inclusive approach to underwriting—one that recognizes the diverse ways people earn income in today's economy. This book will also explore the importance of liquidity and reserves in jumbo lending. When dealing with higher loan amounts, lenders place significant emphasis on a borrower's ability to weather financial fluctuations. This is measured not just by income, but by the availability of assets that can support mortgage payments over time. Understanding how to position your reserves, whether through bank accounts, investment portfolios, or other liquid assets, can dramatically strengthen your application and improve your chances of approval.

In addition to liquidity, credit profile plays a crucial role in jumbo bank statement loans. While these programs offer flexibility in income documentation, they often require stronger credit performance to offset the increased risk associated with higher loan amounts. This does not mean that borrowers need perfect credit, but it does mean that understanding how credit impacts your approval—and how to optimize your credit profile before applying—can make a significant difference. Throughout this book, you will gain insight into how lenders evaluate credit within the context of jumbo lending and how to position yourself accordingly.

Another critical component of jumbo financing is property type and valuation. High-value properties often come with unique characteristics, whether it is location, size, luxury features, or market demand. These factors can influence how a property is appraised and how lenders perceive its risk. Understanding how to select properties that align with lender guidelines, and how to navigate potential appraisal challenges, is an essential part of the jumbo loan process.

Beyond the technical aspects, this book is also about mindset. Stepping into the world of high-value real estate requires a shift in how you view both opportunity and risk. It requires confidence in your financial position, clarity in your strategy, and a willingness to take calculated steps toward larger goals. Jumbo bank statement loans are not just a financing tool—they are a pathway to building long-term wealth, creating stability, and accessing opportunities that can have a lasting impact on your financial future.

Throughout the chapters that follow, you will gain a deep understanding of how jumbo bank statement loans are structured, how lenders evaluate risk, and how you can position yourself for success. You will learn how to analyze your own financial profile, identify strengths and weaknesses, and implement strategies that improve your approval potential. You will also explore real-world scenarios that demonstrate how these loans are used in practice, giving you a clear picture of what is possible when the right strategies are applied. The goal of this book is not just to educate you, but to empower you. By the time you reach the final chapter, you will have the knowledge and confidence to navigate the jumbo lending landscape with precision. You will understand how to communicate effectively with lenders, how to present your financials in the strongest possible light, and how to make informed decisions that align with your long-term objectives.

Jumbo bank statement mortgage loans represent one of the most powerful tools available to modern borrowers. They combine flexibility with opportunity, allowing individuals who have built successful businesses, careers, and investment portfolios to leverage their true income potential. In a world where financial success often looks different from the traditional model, these loans provide a bridge between where you are and where you want to be.

As you begin this journey, remember that the key to success lies in preparation, strategy, and execution. The more you understand the process, the more control you have over the outcome. This book is your guide to mastering that process, unlocking new possibilities, and stepping confidently into the world of high-value real estate financing using bank statement income.

Chapter 1

Understanding Jumbo Bank Statement Mortgage Loan Fundamentals

Jumbo bank statement mortgage loans represent a powerful intersection between high-value real estate financing and flexible income qualification. To fully understand how these loans work, it is essential to first grasp what separates them from both conventional mortgages and standard non-QM bank statement loans. At their core, jumbo loans are designed for properties that exceed conforming loan limits set by agencies such as Fannie Mae and Freddie Mac. Because these loans cannot be sold to these entities, lenders retain more risk, which results in stricter underwriting standards, higher scrutiny, and a greater emphasis on the borrower's overall financial strength. When bank statement income is introduced into this equation, the complexity increases—but so does the opportunity.

The defining characteristic of a jumbo bank statement loan is its ability to qualify borrowers using actual cash flow rather than tax returns. For many high-income individuals, especially business owners and entrepreneurs, tax returns often do not reflect true earning power due to strategic deductions and reinvestments. Traditional underwriting may view these borrowers as lower income, even when their bank accounts tell a very different story. Jumbo bank statement loans solve this problem by analyzing deposits over a period of twelve or twenty-four months, allowing lenders to calculate an average monthly income that better represents real financial activity.

However, unlike standard bank statement loans, jumbo versions demand a higher level of consistency and documentation. Lenders are not only verifying that deposits exist, but also that they are stable, recurring, and derived from legitimate business or personal income sources. Large, unexplained deposits, irregular income patterns, or excessive transfers between accounts can raise red flags. This is why understanding how to structure your accounts and maintain clean financial records is critical when preparing for a jumbo bank statement loan application.

One of the most important concepts in jumbo lending is loan size and its impact on risk. As loan amounts increase, lenders become more cautious. A borrower seeking a $300,000 loan is evaluated differently than one seeking a $1.5 million loan. The higher the loan amount, the greater the lender's exposure, which means every aspect of the borrower's profile must be stronger. This includes credit score, reserves, income stability, and overall financial history. Jumbo bank statement loans are not about meeting minimum requirements—they are about presenting a compelling case that demonstrates financial strength and reliability.

Another critical factor is loan-to-value ratio, commonly referred to as LTV. In jumbo lending, LTV thresholds are often lower than in conforming loans. This means borrowers are typically required to put more money down. For example, while a conventional loan might allow 5% or 10% down, a jumbo bank statement loan may require 20% or more, depending on the lender and the borrower's profile. This larger down payment reduces the lender's risk and demonstrates the borrower's financial commitment to the transaction.

Debt-to-income ratio, or DTI, is another key component, but it is calculated differently in bank statement loans. Instead of using tax returns, lenders derive income from average monthly deposits and then apply an expense factor, especially for business accounts. This expense factor accounts for the cost of running a business and can vary widely depending on the industry. Some lenders use standardized expense ratios, while others allow CPA-prepared profit and loss statements to justify lower expense assumptions. Understanding how these calculations work can significantly impact your qualifying income and, ultimately, your loan approval.

Credit plays a central role in jumbo bank statement lending. Because lenders are taking on higher risk, they often require stronger credit profiles. While exact requirements vary, many jumbo programs look for credit scores in the high 600s to mid-700s or higher. A strong credit history not only improves approval chances but can also lead to better interest rates and loan terms. Conversely, borrowers with lower credit scores may still qualify but will likely face stricter requirements in other areas, such as higher reserves or larger down payments.

Reserves are another defining feature of jumbo loans. Reserves refer to the amount of liquid assets a borrower has available after closing, typically measured in months of mortgage payments. For jumbo bank statement loans, reserve requirements can be substantial, often ranging from six to twelve months or more. These reserves provide lenders with confidence that the borrower can continue making payments even if income fluctuates. For high-value loans, this cushion becomes an essential part of the risk assessment.

In addition to financial metrics, lenders also evaluate the borrower's overall profile. This includes employment history, business stability, and the nature of income sources. For self-employed borrowers, demonstrating a stable or growing business is crucial. Lenders want to see that the income reflected in bank statements is sustainable and not the result of temporary or inconsistent activity. This is why maintaining organized records and a clear financial narrative is so important.

Property type also plays a role in jumbo bank statement loans. High-value properties can vary widely, from luxury primary residences to upscale investment properties. Lenders assess not only the borrower but also the property itself, considering factors such as location, market demand, and appraisal value. Unique or highly specialized properties may present additional challenges, as they can be harder to appraise and sell in the event of default. Understanding how property characteristics impact loan approval is an important part of the jumbo lending process.

Another layer of complexity comes from lender overlays. Unlike conforming loans, which follow standardized guidelines, jumbo loans are heavily influenced by individual lender requirements. These overlays can affect everything from acceptable income calculations to maximum loan amounts and reserve requirements. This variability means that a borrower who is declined by one lender may be approved by another. Navigating this landscape requires both knowledge and strategy, as finding the right lender can make all the difference.

Jumbo bank statement loans also introduce the concept of risk layering. This refers to the combination of multiple risk factors within a single loan file. For example, a high loan amount combined with a lower credit score and limited reserves may be considered too risky. However, if one or more of these factors are strengthened—such as increasing reserves or improving credit—the overall risk profile improves. Understanding how these factors interact allows borrowers to make strategic decisions that enhance their approval potential.

As we move deeper into this book, you will begin to see that jumbo bank statement lending is not simply about meeting guidelines—it is about positioning. Every aspect of your financial profile can be optimized to create a stronger, more compelling application. This includes structuring your bank accounts, managing your deposits, improving your credit, and building reserves. When these elements are aligned, they create a powerful foundation for approval, even at higher loan amounts.

Ultimately, jumbo bank statement mortgage loans represent an opportunity for borrowers who have outgrown traditional lending models. They provide a pathway to high-value real estate by recognizing the true financial strength of individuals whose income does not fit neatly into conventional documentation. By understanding the fundamentals outlined in this chapter, you are taking the first step toward mastering this powerful financing tool and unlocking new levels of opportunity in your real estate journey.

Real-Life Math Example: Jumbo Bank Statement Loan Qualification Scenario

Imagine a borrower named Michael, a self-employed business owner who operates a successful digital marketing agency. Michael is looking to purchase a luxury home priced at $1,500,000. He has strong cash flow, but his tax returns show significantly reduced income due to business deductions. As a result, he decides to pursue a jumbo bank statement mortgage loan.

Michael provides twelve months of business bank statements. Over this period, his total deposits equal $1,200,000. To determine his average monthly income, the lender divides the total deposits by twelve months, resulting in $100,000 per month in gross deposits. However, because this is a business account, the lender applies an expense factor to account for operational costs. In this case, the lender uses a 50% expense ratio, meaning Michael's qualifying income is reduced to $50,000 per month.

Next, the lender evaluates Michael's proposed housing payment. Based on the loan amount, interest rate, property taxes, and insurance, his total monthly housing expense is estimated at $12,000. To calculate his debt-to-income ratio, the lender compares his total monthly obligations to his qualifying income. Michael has an additional $3,000 in monthly debt payments, bringing his total monthly obligations to $15,000. Dividing $15,000 by $50,000 results in a DTI of 30%, which falls well within acceptable limits for many jumbo programs.

The lender then assesses Michael's down payment and loan-to-value ratio. Michael plans to put down 25%, or $375,000, resulting in a loan amount of $1,125,000. This creates an LTV of 75%, which aligns with many jumbo lending guidelines. The lower LTV reduces risk and strengthens his application.

Next, the lender reviews Michael's reserves. After accounting for his down payment and closing costs, Michael has $200,000 remaining in liquid assets. With a monthly housing payment of $12,000, this equates to approximately sixteen months of reserves, which exceeds typical requirements for jumbo loans. This strong reserve position serves as a significant compensating factor.

Credit is another important component. Michael has a credit score of 720, with a solid history of on-time payments and low credit utilization. This places him in a favorable position, as many jumbo programs prefer scores above 700. His strong credit profile further enhances his overall risk assessment.

The lender also examines the consistency of Michael's deposits. His bank statements show regular, recurring income from multiple clients, with no large unexplained deposits. This consistency reinforces the reliability of his income and supports the lender's confidence in his ability to repay the loan.

After reviewing all aspects of Michael's application—income, DTI, LTV, reserves, credit, and deposit consistency—the lender determines that he meets the requirements for a jumbo bank statement mortgage loan. Despite his tax returns showing lower income, his true financial strength is captured through his bank statements, allowing him to qualify for the financing needed to purchase his desired property.

This example illustrates how jumbo bank statement loans operate in practice. By focusing on actual cash flow and combining it with strong compensating factors, borrowers like Michael can access high-value real estate opportunities that would otherwise be out of reach. Understanding these calculations and how each component contributes to the overall approval process is essential for anyone looking to succeed in jumbo bank statement lending.

Chapter 2

Jumbo Loan Limits, Overlays, and How Lenders Evaluate Risk at Higher Loan Amounts

As you move deeper into the world of jumbo bank statement mortgage loans, one of the most important shifts you must make is understanding that higher loan amounts bring a completely different level of scrutiny. In traditional mortgage lending, many borrowers rely on standardized guidelines that are widely accepted across lenders. However, once a loan exceeds conforming limits, the rules change. Jumbo loans exist outside the boundaries of agency-backed financing, meaning lenders must rely on their own internal risk models, policies, and investor requirements. This is where the concept of overlays becomes central to your success.

Loan limits are the starting point. Conforming loans are capped at limits set annually by entities such as Fannie Mae and Freddie Mac. Any loan amount that exceeds these limits is considered jumbo. While this may seem like a simple threshold, crossing into jumbo territory fundamentally changes how your loan is evaluated. Lenders are no longer able to offload the risk to government-sponsored enterprises, which means they must ensure that every aspect of the borrower's profile supports the increased exposure.

In jumbo lending, risk is not assessed through a single metric—it is evaluated holistically. Lenders look at the entire financial picture and weigh each component against the others. This includes income stability, credit strength, liquidity, property value, and borrower experience. At higher loan amounts, even small weaknesses can become magnified. For example, a slightly elevated debt-to-income ratio that might be acceptable in a conforming loan could become a concern in a jumbo scenario. This is why understanding how lenders think is just as important as understanding the guidelines themselves.

Overlays are the additional requirements that lenders impose on top of baseline guidelines. These can vary significantly from one lender to another, and they are often influenced by the lender's risk tolerance, investor relationships, and market conditions. One lender may allow a higher loan-to-value ratio for a borrower with strong reserves, while another may require a lower LTV regardless of other strengths. Similarly, some lenders may accept a wider range of income documentation, while others may be more conservative in how they calculate qualifying income. This variability creates both challenges and opportunities. On one hand, it can be frustrating for borrowers who receive different answers from different lenders. On the other hand, it means that there is rarely a single "yes" or "no" answer. Instead, there is often a path to approval—it simply requires finding the right lender whose guidelines align with your financial profile. This is why working with experienced professionals who understand the jumbo landscape can be a significant advantage.

One of the key areas where overlays come into play is loan-to-value ratio. While some jumbo programs may advertise maximum LTVs of 80% or even higher, these limits are often reserved for borrowers with exceptionally strong profiles. In practice, many lenders prefer lower LTVs, especially when other risk factors are present. A borrower with a higher credit score, strong reserves, and consistent income may be able to qualify at a higher LTV, while a borrower with weaker compensating factors may be required to put more money down.

Debt-to-income ratio is another area where overlays can vary. In bank statement loans, DTI is already more complex due to the way income is calculated. When combined with jumbo loan amounts, lenders often become more conservative. Some may cap DTI at 40% or lower, while others may allow higher ratios if the borrower demonstrates strong compensating factors. Understanding where your DTI falls and how it interacts with other elements of your profile is critical when navigating jumbo lending.

Liquidity and reserves are perhaps the most influential factors in jumbo loan approvals. At higher loan amounts, lenders want to see that borrowers have the financial capacity to sustain their obligations over time. This is not just about having enough money to close—it is about having enough money to continue making payments even in the face of income fluctuations. Reserve requirements can vary widely, but it is not uncommon for jumbo lenders to require twelve months or more of reserves, particularly for investment properties or higher-risk profiles.

Credit overlays also play a significant role. While bank statement loans offer flexibility in income documentation, they often require stronger credit profiles to offset that flexibility. Many jumbo programs set minimum credit score thresholds, and higher scores can unlock better terms and more favorable guidelines. However, credit is not evaluated in isolation. Lenders also consider payment history, credit utilization, and the overall structure of the borrower's credit profile.

Another important concept in jumbo lending is risk layering. This refers to the presence of multiple risk factors within a single loan file. For example, a high loan amount combined with a high LTV, lower credit score, and limited reserves would be considered a layered risk scenario. In such cases, lenders may either decline the loan or require adjustments to reduce risk. This could involve increasing the down payment, improving credit, or demonstrating additional liquidity. Understanding how to minimize risk layering is a key strategy for achieving approval.

Property evaluation becomes more nuanced in jumbo loans as well. High-value properties are often unique, and their marketability can impact lender decisions. A luxury property in a desirable location with strong demand is viewed differently than a highly specialized property in a niche market. Lenders want to ensure that the property can be sold if necessary, which is why appraisal quality and market analysis are critical components of the approval process.

Another layer to consider is the influence of market conditions. Jumbo lending is closely tied to broader economic factors, including interest rates, housing market trends, and investor appetite. During periods of economic uncertainty, lenders may tighten guidelines and increase overlays. Conversely, in strong markets, they may become more flexible. Staying informed about these trends can help you time your application and position yourself more effectively.

As you begin to understand how overlays and risk evaluation work, you will see that jumbo lending is not about fitting into a rigid box—it is about building a strong, well-balanced profile. Each component of your financial picture contributes to the overall assessment, and strengths in one area can offset weaknesses in another. This is where strategy becomes essential. By proactively managing your finances and understanding how lenders evaluate risk, you can significantly improve your chances of approval.

Ultimately, jumbo bank statement mortgage loans require a higher level of preparation, awareness, and execution. They demand that borrowers take an active role in shaping their financial profile and presenting it in the strongest possible light. By mastering the concepts outlined in this chapter, you will be better equipped to navigate the complexities of jumbo lending and position yourself for success at higher loan amounts.

Real-Life Math Example: Navigating Jumbo Overlays and Risk Factors

Consider a borrower named Sophia, who is looking to purchase a high-end property priced at $2,000,000. She is a self-employed consultant with strong cash flow but limited taxable income due to business deductions. Sophia decides to pursue a jumbo bank statement mortgage loan.

Sophia provides twenty-four months of personal bank statements showing total deposits of $1,920,000. When divided over twenty-four months, this results in an average monthly income of $80,000. Because these are personal accounts, no expense factor is applied, allowing her to use the full amount as qualifying income.

Her proposed monthly housing payment, including principal, interest, taxes, and insurance, is $14,000. She also has $4,000 in monthly debt obligations, bringing her total monthly obligations to $18,000. Dividing $18,000 by her $80,000 monthly income results in a DTI of 22.5%, which is well within acceptable limits for most jumbo programs.

Sophia plans to put down 20%, or $400,000, resulting in a loan amount of $1,600,000 and an LTV of 80%. While this meets the maximum LTV for some jumbo programs, her lender applies an overlay requiring a lower LTV for loans above $1.5 million. As a result, the lender requests that Sophia increase her down payment to 25%, or $500,000, reducing the loan amount to $1,500,000 and the LTV to 75%.

Next, the lender evaluates Sophia's reserves. After her down payment and closing costs, she has $150,000 remaining in liquid assets. With a monthly housing payment of $14,000, this equates to just over ten months of reserves. However, the lender's overlay requires twelve months of reserves for loans above $1.5 million. To meet this requirement, Sophia decides to move additional funds from an investment account, increasing her reserves to $200,000, or approximately fourteen months.

Sophia's credit score is 690, which meets the minimum requirement for some programs but falls short of the lender's preferred threshold of 700 for jumbo loans at this level. To address this, Sophia pays down several credit card balances, reducing her utilization and increasing her score to 710. This improvement strengthens her profile and aligns with the lender's expectations.

The lender also reviews her deposit history and notes consistent income from multiple sources, with no significant irregularities. This consistency supports the stability of her income and reinforces the overall strength of her application.

Initially, Sophia's loan application faced challenges due to overlays related to LTV, reserves, and credit score. However, by making strategic adjustments—such as increasing her down payment, boosting her reserves, and improving her credit—she was able to align her profile with the lender's requirements. These changes reduced risk and demonstrated her financial strength, ultimately leading to loan approval.

This example highlights the importance of understanding overlays and how they impact jumbo loan approvals. It shows that even strong borrowers may need to make adjustments to meet lender-specific requirements. By recognizing these factors and taking proactive steps, borrowers can navigate the complexities of jumbo lending and achieve successful outcomes.

Chapter 3

Structuring Income for Jumbo Bank Statement Loan Approval

When it comes to jumbo bank statement mortgage loans, income is not just something you document—it is something you engineer. Unlike traditional lending, where income is extracted directly from tax returns and W-2 forms, bank statement loans require a deeper level of interpretation. Lenders are not simply verifying what you earn; they are analyzing how your income flows, how consistent it is, and how reliably it can support a large financial obligation. At the jumbo level, this analysis becomes even more critical, because the stakes are higher and the margin for error is smaller.

The foundation of income structuring begins with understanding how lenders calculate qualifying income from bank statements. Typically, lenders will take twelve or twenty-four months of deposits and average them to determine a monthly income figure. For personal bank statements, this process is relatively straightforward. Deposits are totaled and divided over the number of months provided. However, for business bank statements, lenders apply an expense factor to account for operating costs. This factor can range from as low as 10% to as high as 75%, depending on the lender and the nature of the business. The higher the expense factor, the lower the qualifying income.

This is where strategy comes into play. Borrowers who understand how expense factors are applied can position themselves to maximize qualifying income. For example, some lenders allow the use of a CPA-prepared profit and loss statement to justify a lower expense ratio. This can significantly increase qualifying income and improve approval chances. Without this knowledge, a borrower might unknowingly accept a higher expense factor that reduces their income and limits their borrowing power.

Another key aspect of income structuring is consistency. Jumbo lenders are highly sensitive to fluctuations in income, especially when qualifying based on deposits. Large spikes followed by periods of lower activity can raise concerns about stability. Lenders want to see a predictable pattern of income that demonstrates the borrower's ability to sustain payments over time. This means that managing the timing and flow of deposits can have a direct impact on how your income is perceived.

For self-employed borrowers, separating personal and business finances is critical. Mixing accounts can create confusion and make it more difficult for lenders to accurately assess income. Clean, well-organized accounts not only simplify the underwriting process but also present a more professional and reliable financial profile. When deposits are clearly tied to business activity, lenders are more confident in their legitimacy and consistency.

Another important factor is the source of deposits. Lenders must verify that income is derived from acceptable and recurring sources. This includes revenue from business operations, client payments, and other consistent income streams. Non-recurring deposits, such as one-time transfers, gifts, or asset sales, are typically excluded from income calculations. Understanding this distinction allows borrowers to focus on building a deposit history that aligns with lender expectations.

Timing also plays a significant role in income structuring. The period leading up to your loan application is crucial, as lenders will be analyzing recent financial activity. This means that strategic planning should begin well in advance. By maintaining consistent deposits, avoiding large unexplained transactions, and ensuring that accounts reflect stable income, borrowers can create a stronger foundation for approval.

In jumbo lending, income alone is not enough. It must be supported by other elements of the borrower's profile, including credit, reserves, and overall financial stability. This is where the concept of compensating factors becomes important. A borrower with slightly lower qualifying income may still be approved if they demonstrate strong reserves, excellent credit, or a low loan-to-value ratio. Conversely, a borrower with high income but weak supporting factors may face challenges.

Another layer of complexity comes from multiple income streams. Many self-employed borrowers generate income from various sources, including multiple businesses, investments, or side ventures. While this can strengthen the overall financial picture, it can also complicate the underwriting process. Lenders must verify each income source and ensure that it is stable and consistent. Proper documentation and organization are essential when presenting multiple streams of income.

It is also important to understand how lenders treat declining or increasing income trends. A declining trend may raise concerns about future stability, even if current income levels are sufficient. On the other hand, an increasing trend can be viewed positively, as it suggests growth and improving financial strength. However, lenders will still look for consistency and may average income over the entire period rather than focusing solely on recent increases.

Another strategic consideration is the use of business versus personal bank statements. In some cases, using personal accounts may result in higher qualifying income, as no expense factor is applied. In other cases, business accounts combined with a favorable expense ratio may produce better results. The choice depends on the borrower's specific financial situation and how income flows through their accounts.

Documentation plays a critical role in income structuring. Lenders may request additional information to verify the nature of deposits, such as invoices, contracts, or business licenses. Being prepared to provide this documentation can streamline the approval process and reduce delays. It also reinforces the credibility of the borrower's income.

As loan amounts increase, lenders may apply additional scrutiny to income calculations. This includes verifying that deposits are not artificially inflated and that they accurately reflect ongoing business activity. Any inconsistencies or irregularities can lead to additional questions or even denial. This is why transparency and accuracy are essential when preparing your financial profile.

Another important concept is scalability. Borrowers who are looking to grow their real estate portfolio or move into higher price points must think beyond a single transaction. Structuring income in a way that supports long-term growth can create opportunities for future financing. This means building a financial profile that is not only strong today but sustainable over time.

Ultimately, structuring income for jumbo bank statement loan approval is both an art and a science. It requires a deep understanding of how lenders evaluate income, combined with strategic planning and execution. By taking control of how your income is presented and ensuring that it aligns with lender expectations, you can significantly increase your chances of approval and unlock access to higher-value real estate opportunities.

Real-Life Math Example: Structuring Income for Maximum Qualification

Consider a borrower named Daniel, a self-employed entrepreneur who owns two businesses: a consulting firm and an e-commerce company. Daniel is looking to purchase a luxury property priced at $1,800,000 and plans to use a jumbo bank statement mortgage loan.

Daniel provides twelve months of business bank statements for both companies. His consulting firm shows total deposits of $720,000 over twelve months, while his e-commerce business shows $480,000 in deposits over the same period. Combined, his total annual deposits equal $1,200,000, which averages to $100,000 per month.

However, because these are business accounts, the lender applies an expense factor. Initially, the lender uses a standard 50% expense ratio, reducing Daniel's qualifying income to $50,000 per month. Based on this income, Daniel's debt-to-income ratio exceeds the lender's limit, making it difficult for him to qualify for the desired loan amount.

Daniel then works with a CPA to prepare a detailed profit and loss statement that shows his actual business expenses are closer to 30%. The lender agrees to use this lower expense ratio, increasing his qualifying income to $70,000 per month. This adjustment significantly improves his DTI and brings it within acceptable limits.

Next, Daniel evaluates his deposit consistency. While his consulting income is stable, his e-commerce business shows seasonal fluctuations, with higher deposits during certain months. To address this, the lender averages income over the full twelve-month period, smoothing out the fluctuations and providing a more consistent income figure.

Daniel also reviews his bank statements for non-recurring deposits. He identifies several large transfers between accounts and provides documentation to clarify that these are internal transfers, not additional income. The lender excludes these amounts from the income calculation, ensuring accuracy. To further strengthen his profile, Daniel decides to include personal bank statements that show additional income from investment distributions. These deposits add $5,000 per month to his qualifying income, increasing his total to $75,000 per month.

With this adjusted income, Daniel's monthly housing payment of $13,500 and additional debts of $3,500 result in total obligations of $17,000. Dividing $17,000 by $75,000 produces a DTI of approximately 22.7%, which is well within acceptable limits for jumbo loans.

Daniel also ensures that his deposits remain consistent in the months leading up to his application. He avoids large irregular transactions and maintains a steady flow of income, reinforcing the stability of his financial profile.

By strategically structuring his income—reducing the expense factor, combining multiple income sources, and ensuring consistency—Daniel transforms a challenging scenario into a strong loan application. His understanding of how lenders evaluate bank statement income allows him to maximize his qualifying income and secure approval for his jumbo mortgage.

This example demonstrates that income structuring is not just about what you earn, but how you present it. By taking a proactive approach and aligning your financial profile with lender expectations, you can significantly enhance your borrowing power and achieve your real estate goals.

Chapter 4

Credit, Reserves, and Compensating Factors in Jumbo Bank Statement Loans

As you advance into the world of jumbo bank statement mortgage loans, you begin to realize that income alone is never enough. While structuring income properly is a critical foundation, it is only one piece of a much larger puzzle. In jumbo lending, especially when using alternative documentation like bank statements, lenders rely heavily on what are known as compensating factors. These are the strengths within your financial profile that offset perceived risks and provide confidence to the lender that you can successfully repay a large loan over time. Among these, credit and reserves stand out as two of the most powerful and influential components.

Credit is often the first filter through which jumbo loan applications are evaluated. Unlike conforming loans, where automated underwriting systems may provide approvals based on standardized criteria, jumbo loans are frequently underwritten manually or through more conservative internal models. This means that your credit profile is examined in detail—not just your score, but your entire credit behavior. Lenders are looking for patterns of responsibility, consistency, and financial discipline. A high credit score is not just a number; it is a reflection of how you manage debt, how reliably you make payments, and how you handle financial obligations over time.

In jumbo bank statement loans, credit becomes even more important because income documentation is less traditional. Since lenders are not relying on tax returns, they need additional assurance that the borrower is financially responsible. A strong credit profile helps provide that assurance. Typically, borrowers with scores in the 700+ range are viewed more favorably, but approval is not limited to those with perfect credit. What matters most is the overall story your credit profile tells. A borrower with a 720 score and a clean payment history will often be seen as lower risk than someone with a higher score but inconsistent behavior.

Another key aspect of credit evaluation is credit utilization. This refers to how much of your available credit you are currently using. High utilization can signal financial stress, even if payments are made on time. For jumbo loans, lenders often prefer to see lower utilization levels, as this indicates that the borrower has access to credit but is not overly reliant on it. Reducing credit card balances before applying can have a significant impact on both your score and your overall risk profile.

In addition to utilization, lenders examine the depth and age of your credit history. A longer credit history with a mix of accounts—such as credit cards, installment loans, and mortgages—demonstrates experience in managing different types of debt. This diversity can strengthen your application, especially in jumbo lending, where lenders are looking for borrowers who have successfully handled significant financial responsibilities in the past.

While credit establishes trust, reserves provide security. Reserves refer to the liquid assets you have available after closing, and they are a cornerstone of jumbo loan approvals. At higher loan amounts, lenders want to know that you have the financial cushion to continue making payments even if your income fluctuates. This is particularly important for self-employed borrowers, whose income may not be as predictable as that of salaried employees.

Reserve requirements in jumbo bank statement loans are often more substantial than in conventional loans. It is not uncommon for lenders to require twelve months or more of reserves, especially for larger loan amounts or investment properties. These reserves can be held in various forms, including checking and savings accounts, money market funds, stocks, and other liquid assets. The key is that they must be accessible and verifiable.

The strength of your reserves can significantly influence your loan approval. A borrower with strong reserves may be approved even if other aspects of their profile are slightly weaker. For example, a borrower with a higher debt-to-income ratio or a lower credit score may still qualify if they demonstrate significant liquidity. This is the essence of compensating factors—strengths in one area offsetting weaknesses in another.

Another important consideration is how reserves are calculated. Lenders typically express reserves in terms of months of housing payments. For example, if your monthly mortgage payment is $10,000 and you have $120,000 in liquid assets, you have twelve months of reserves. Understanding this calculation allows you to plan strategically and ensure that you meet or exceed lender requirements.

Compensating factors extend beyond credit and reserves. They include any element of your financial profile that reduces risk in the eyes of the lender. This can include a low loan-to-value ratio, stable and consistent income, a strong employment or business history, and even the type of property being financed.

Each of these factors contributes to the overall assessment of your application. One of the most powerful compensating factors is a larger down payment. By reducing the loan-to-value ratio, you decrease the lender's exposure and demonstrate a higher level of financial commitment. In jumbo lending, where loan amounts are significant, this can have a profound impact on approval. A borrower who increases their down payment from 20% to 30% may significantly improve their chances of approval, even if other aspects of their profile are not perfect.

Another compensating factor is the stability of your income. Even when using bank statements, lenders look for consistency and predictability. A borrower with steady deposits over time is viewed more favorably than one with irregular or volatile income. This stability reassures lenders that the borrower can maintain their financial obligations over the long term.

Business strength also plays a role, particularly for self-employed borrowers. Lenders may consider the longevity of your business, the industry you operate in, and the overall trajectory of your income. A well-established business with a history of growth is a strong indicator of future stability, which can enhance your application.

It is also important to understand how these factors interact. Jumbo lending is not about meeting a single requirement—it is about balancing multiple elements to create a strong overall profile. A borrower with slightly weaker credit but strong reserves and a low LTV may be approved, while another borrower with higher credit but limited reserves may face challenges. The key is to identify your strengths and leverage them effectively.

Timing is another critical factor. Preparing your credit and reserves well in advance of your loan application can make a significant difference. Paying down debt, increasing savings, and organizing your financial accounts are all steps that can strengthen your profile and improve your chances of approval. Jumbo loans reward preparation and strategic planning.

As you continue through this journey, it becomes clear that jumbo bank statement loans are not just about qualifying—they are about positioning yourself as a low-risk, high-confidence borrower. By understanding how credit, reserves, and compensating factors influence lender decisions, you gain the ability to shape your financial profile in a way that aligns with approval criteria.

Ultimately, this chapter highlights a fundamental truth: lenders are not just evaluating numbers—they are evaluating risk. Your job is to present a financial story that minimizes that risk and maximizes confidence. When you do this effectively, you unlock the ability to secure financing at higher levels and move forward with your real estate goals.

Real-Life Math Example: Using Credit, Reserves, and Compensating Factors to Secure Approval

Consider a borrower named Olivia, a self-employed interior designer looking to purchase a luxury home priced at $1,700,000. She plans to use a jumbo bank statement mortgage loan and has already structured her income effectively. However, her approval depends heavily on how she manages her credit, reserves, and compensating factors.

Olivia's qualifying income, based on bank statements, is $65,000 per month. Her proposed monthly housing payment is $13,000, and she has additional monthly debts totaling $4,000. This brings her total monthly obligations to $17,000. Dividing $17,000 by $65,000 results in a debt-to-income ratio of approximately 26.1%, which is within acceptable limits for jumbo loans.

However, Olivia's credit score is 680, which is slightly below the preferred threshold for many jumbo programs. While this does not automatically disqualify her, it does introduce additional risk. To compensate, Olivia focuses on strengthening other areas of her profile.

She begins by reducing her credit card balances, lowering her utilization from 60% to 25%. This action increases her credit score to 705, moving her into a more favorable range. This improvement not only strengthens her application but may also result in better loan terms.

Next, Olivia evaluates her reserves. After accounting for her down payment and closing costs, she has $100,000 in liquid assets. With a monthly housing payment of $13,000, this equates to approximately 7.7 months of reserves. However, her lender requires a minimum of twelve months for this loan size.

To address this, Olivia transfers additional funds from an investment account, increasing her total reserves to $180,000. This provides nearly fourteen months of reserves, exceeding the lender's requirement and serving as a strong compensating factor.

Olivia also decides to increase her down payment. Initially, she planned to put down 20%, or $340,000, resulting in an 80% LTV. By increasing her down payment to 25%, or $425,000, she reduces her loan amount and lowers her LTV to 75%. This reduction in risk further strengthens her application.

With these adjustments, Olivia's profile now includes a strong credit score, substantial reserves, and a lower LTV. These compensating factors offset any initial concerns and present her as a low-risk borrower. The lender reviews her application and determines that, despite the initial credit score challenge, her overall financial profile is strong. Her reserves provide a significant safety net, her improved credit demonstrates responsibility, and her lower LTV reduces exposure. As a result, she is approved for the jumbo bank statement mortgage loan.

This example illustrates how credit, reserves, and compensating factors work together to influence loan approval. It shows that even when one aspect of a borrower's profile is not ideal, strategic adjustments can create a balanced and compelling application. By understanding and applying these principles, borrowers can navigate the complexities of jumbo lending and achieve successful outcomes.

Chapter 5
Jumbo Bank Statement Mortgage Loans for Primary Residences

When it comes to financing a primary residence using a jumbo bank statement mortgage loan, the stakes are both financial and personal. Unlike investment properties, which are often evaluated primarily through numbers and performance metrics, a primary residence represents stability, lifestyle, and long-term commitment. For lenders, this distinction matters. Borrowers are statistically more likely to prioritize payments on their primary home over any other obligation. Because of this, jumbo bank statement loans for primary residences often come with slightly more flexibility compared to investment scenarios—but they still require a high level of financial strength and strategic preparation.

At the jumbo level, primary residence financing introduces a unique combination of opportunity and responsibility. Borrowers are typically seeking higher-priced homes in desirable locations, often upgrading their lifestyle or securing a long-term family residence. These properties come with larger loan amounts, higher monthly payments, and stricter underwriting standards. When bank statement income is used instead of tax returns, lenders must carefully evaluate whether the borrower's actual cash flow can support these obligations consistently over time.

One of the first distinctions in primary residence jumbo loans is how occupancy impacts risk. Lenders view owner-occupied properties as lower risk compared to second homes or investment properties. This is because borrowers are more emotionally and financially invested in their primary residence. As a result, lenders may allow slightly higher loan-to-value ratios, more flexible debt-to-income thresholds, and in some cases, lower reserve requirements compared to other property types. However, these allowances are still balanced by the overall risk profile of the borrower.

Loan-to-value ratio remains a central component of jumbo lending. For primary residences, many lenders offer maximum LTVs ranging from 75% to 85%, depending on the borrower's strength. However, higher LTVs are typically reserved for borrowers with excellent credit, strong reserves, and consistent income. For most borrowers using bank statement loans, a 20% to 25% down payment is common. This not only reduces the lender's risk but also strengthens the borrower's position during underwriting.

Another critical factor is the borrower's monthly housing expense, often referred to as the total housing payment. This includes principal, interest, property taxes, homeowners insurance, and any applicable association dues. In jumbo loans, especially for high-value properties, this payment can be substantial. Lenders must ensure that the borrower's income—calculated from bank statements—can comfortably support this expense without creating financial strain.

Debt-to-income ratio is evaluated carefully in primary residence jumbo loans. While some flexibility exists, lenders typically prefer DTIs below 43%, with many favoring even lower ratios for higher loan amounts. Because bank statement income can fluctuate, lenders often take a conservative approach when calculating qualifying income. This makes it essential for borrowers to present consistent deposits and avoid irregularities that could reduce their qualifying income.

Reserves continue to play a major role, even for primary residences. While requirements may be slightly lower than for investment properties, lenders still expect borrowers to have a significant financial cushion. This is especially important for self-employed individuals, whose income may vary from month to month. Demonstrating strong reserves reassures lenders that the borrower can maintain payments even during periods of reduced income. Credit requirements for jumbo primary residence loans are generally strong, though not necessarily perfect. Borrowers with scores above 700 are typically viewed more favorably, but those with slightly lower scores may still qualify if they present strong compensating factors. As with all jumbo loans, credit is evaluated in context. A borrower with solid payment history, low utilization, and established credit depth can offset a slightly lower score.

Another important consideration is the stability of the borrower's lifestyle and financial profile. Lenders often look at factors such as length of time in business, consistency of income, and overall financial behavior. For primary residences, there is an added emphasis on long-term stability. Lenders want to see that the borrower is not only capable of making payments today but is also likely to maintain that capability in the future.

Property evaluation is also critical. High-value primary residences must meet appraisal standards that support the loan amount. Lenders assess not only the value of the property but also its marketability. A well-located home in a desirable area with strong demand is viewed more favorably than a highly unique or specialized property that may be difficult to sell. This is particularly important in jumbo lending, where the lender's exposure is significantly higher.

Another advantage of primary residence jumbo loans is the potential for more favorable interest rates compared to investment properties. Because of the lower perceived risk, lenders may offer better pricing, especially for borrowers with strong profiles. This can result in significant long-term savings, given the size of jumbo loan balances.

Strategic planning is essential when preparing for a jumbo bank statement loan on a primary residence. Borrowers should focus on maintaining clean and consistent bank statements, optimizing credit, building reserves, and structuring their finances in a way that supports a strong application. Timing is also important, as recent financial activity will carry significant weight during underwriting.

One often overlooked aspect is the psychological component of qualifying for a high-value primary residence. Borrowers must be comfortable with larger monthly obligations and confident in their financial stability. This requires not only strong income but also disciplined financial management. Understanding your numbers, planning for contingencies, and maintaining a long-term perspective are all critical to success.

Another key factor is the alignment between the borrower's income and the property they are purchasing. Lenders assess whether the home is reasonable given the borrower's financial profile. Even if a borrower technically qualifies, a property that appears excessive relative to income and assets may raise concerns. Ensuring that the purchase aligns with your overall financial picture can help avoid unnecessary challenges during underwriting.

As you move forward, it becomes clear that jumbo bank statement loans for primary residences are about more than just qualification—they are about positioning yourself for long-term success. By understanding how lenders evaluate these loans and taking a strategic approach to your finances, you can confidently pursue higher-value properties and create a stable foundation for your future.

Real-Life Math Example: Purchasing a Primary Residence with a Jumbo Bank Statement Loan

Consider a borrower named Anthony, a self-employed software consultant who is looking to purchase a primary residence priced at $1,600,000. Anthony has strong cash flow but writes off a significant portion of his income on tax returns. As a result, he chooses to apply for a jumbo bank statement mortgage loan.

Anthony provides twelve months of personal bank statements showing total deposits of $960,000. Dividing this by twelve months results in an average monthly income of $80,000. Because these are personal accounts, no expense factor is applied, allowing him to use the full amount as qualifying income. Anthony plans to put down 20%, or $320,000, resulting in a loan amount of $1,280,000 and an LTV of 80%. His estimated monthly housing payment, including taxes and insurance, is $12,500. He also has $2,500 in monthly debt obligations, bringing his total monthly obligations to $15,000.

To calculate his debt-to-income ratio, the lender divides $15,000 by his $80,000 monthly income, resulting in a DTI of 18.75%. This low DTI is a strong indicator of his ability to manage the loan.

Next, the lender evaluates Anthony's reserves. After his down payment and closing costs, he has $150,000 remaining in liquid assets. With a monthly housing payment of $12,500, this equates to twelve months of reserves, meeting the lender's requirement.

Anthony's credit score is 730, with a strong history of on-time payments and low utilization. This places him in an excellent position for jumbo lending and may qualify him for favorable interest rates.

The lender also reviews the consistency of Anthony's deposits. His bank statements show regular income from multiple clients, with no large unexplained deposits or irregularities. This consistency reinforces the stability of his income. During underwriting, the lender considers all aspects of Anthony's profile: strong income, low DTI, solid reserves, and excellent credit. These factors combine to create a low-risk profile, even at a high loan amount.

Anthony is approved for the jumbo bank statement mortgage loan and successfully purchases his primary residence. His ability to present a clean and consistent financial profile, combined with strong compensating factors, allows him to qualify for a high-value home without relying on tax returns.

This example demonstrates how jumbo bank statement loans for primary residences work in practice. By understanding how income, credit, reserves, and property factors interact, borrowers can position themselves for approval and confidently move forward with their home purchase.

Chapter 6

Jumbo Bank Statement Mortgage Loans for Investment Properties

As you transition from financing a primary residence into the world of investment properties, the dynamics of jumbo bank statement mortgage loans shift significantly. While primary residence loans benefit from the borrower's emotional attachment and prioritization of payments, investment properties are evaluated through a more analytical lens. Lenders focus heavily on risk, cash flow sustainability, and the borrower's ability to manage multiple financial obligations. When you combine jumbo loan amounts with investment property risk and bank statement income, the level of scrutiny increases—but so does the potential for wealth creation.

Investment properties financed through jumbo bank statement loans are often associated with higher-value rental homes, luxury short-term rentals, multi-unit properties, or high-demand properties in premium markets. These assets are not just places to live—they are vehicles for income generation and long-term appreciation. However, lenders understand that investment properties are more likely to be defaulted on before a primary residence, which is why they apply stricter guidelines in these scenarios. One of the first major differences in investment property jumbo loans is loan-to-value ratio. Compared to primary residences, lenders typically require lower LTVs for investment properties. While a primary residence might allow 80% LTV or higher, investment properties often cap at 70% to 75%, and sometimes even lower depending on the loan size and borrower profile. This means borrowers must bring larger down payments, often ranging from 25% to 30% or more. This increased equity reduces lender risk and ensures the borrower has a significant financial stake in the property.

Debt-to-income ratio is also evaluated more conservatively for investment properties. Because rental income can fluctuate and market conditions can change, lenders want to ensure that borrowers are not over-leveraged. In jumbo bank statement loans, DTI calculations are based on derived income from deposits, which adds another layer of complexity. Lenders may require lower DTIs, often in the range of 40% or below, especially when dealing with higher loan amounts.

Another key factor in investment property lending is reserves. Reserve requirements for jumbo investment loans are typically higher than for primary residences. It is not uncommon for lenders to require twelve to twenty-four months of reserves, particularly for borrowers with multiple properties or higher risk profiles. These reserves must cover not only the subject property but sometimes additional properties owned by the borrower. This ensures that the borrower can sustain multiple mortgage payments even if rental income is temporarily disrupted.

Credit requirements also become more stringent. While primary residence loans may allow some flexibility, investment property jumbo loans often require stronger credit profiles. Lenders want to see a history of responsible financial management, particularly when borrowers are taking on additional properties. Higher credit scores not only improve approval chances but also help secure better interest rates, which can significantly impact long-term profitability.

One of the most important aspects of investment property financing is understanding how income is evaluated. In traditional loans, rental income may be used to offset mortgage payments. However, in bank statement loans, income is primarily derived from deposits, and rental income may or may not be fully considered depending on the lender's guidelines. This is where strategy becomes essential. Borrowers must ensure that their bank statements accurately reflect their income streams, including rental income where applicable.

In some cases, borrowers may combine bank statement income with other qualifying methods, such as debt service coverage ratio (DSCR) strategies. DSCR focuses on the property's ability to generate income relative to its expenses. While this book focuses on bank statement loans, understanding how these strategies can complement each other provides additional flexibility. For example, a borrower may use bank statement income to qualify personally while also demonstrating that the property itself produces sufficient cash flow.

Property type plays a critical role in investment property jumbo loans. Lenders evaluate not only the borrower but also the income potential and marketability of the property. High-end rental properties in desirable locations are viewed more favorably than properties in less stable markets. Short-term rental properties, such as vacation homes, may require additional analysis due to the variability of income. Understanding how property characteristics influence lender decisions is essential when selecting an investment.

Another important concept is portfolio management. Many borrowers seeking jumbo investment loans already own multiple properties. Lenders will evaluate the entire portfolio, including existing mortgage obligations, rental income, and overall financial stability. This means that each new property must fit within the broader financial picture. Overextending your portfolio can increase risk and reduce your chances of approval.

Risk layering becomes particularly important in investment property lending. A high loan amount combined with a high LTV, lower credit score, and limited reserves can create a scenario that lenders are unwilling to approve. However, strengthening one or more of these factors can offset risk. For example, increasing reserves or lowering the LTV can significantly improve the overall profile.

Another key factor is cash flow analysis. While bank statement loans focus on deposits, lenders still want to understand the sustainability of income. This includes evaluating the consistency of deposits, the reliability of income sources, and the borrower's ability to manage expenses. For investment properties, demonstrating positive cash flow—or at least the ability to cover expenses—is critical.

Market conditions also influence investment property lending. In strong real estate markets, lenders may be more flexible, while in uncertain markets, they may tighten guidelines. Understanding these trends can help borrowers make informed decisions about timing and strategy.

One of the most powerful aspects of jumbo bank statement

loans for investment properties is scalability. These loans allow borrowers to leverage their true income potential to acquire higher-value assets. By building a strong financial profile and maintaining disciplined management, borrowers can expand their portfolios and create significant wealth over time.

However, scalability requires careful planning. Each new property adds complexity to your financial profile, and lenders will evaluate how well you manage this growth. Maintaining strong reserves, consistent income, and a balanced portfolio is essential for long-term success.

Ultimately, jumbo bank statement mortgage loans for investment properties represent a strategic opportunity for borrowers who understand how to navigate the complexities of higher-value financing. By aligning your financial profile with lender expectations and taking a disciplined approach to portfolio growth, you can unlock access to premium real estate opportunities and build a foundation for long-term wealth.

Real-Life Math Example: Financing a Jumbo Investment Property

Consider a borrower named Marcus, a self-employed real estate investor who is looking to purchase a luxury rental property priced at $2,200,000. Marcus has a strong portfolio of properties and generates significant income, but his tax returns show lower income due to deductions. He decides to use a jumbo bank statement mortgage loan. Marcus provides twenty-four months of business bank statements showing total deposits of $2,400,000. Dividing this by twenty-four months results in an average monthly income of $100,000. The lender applies a 40% expense factor, reducing his qualifying income to $60,000 per month.

Marcus plans to put down 30%, or $660,000, resulting in a loan amount of $1,540,000 and an LTV of 70%. This lower LTV aligns with lender requirements for investment properties and reduces overall risk.

His estimated monthly housing payment, including taxes and insurance, is $15,000. Marcus also has existing mortgage obligations of $10,000 per month across his portfolio, bringing his total monthly obligations to $25,000.

To calculate his debt-to-income ratio, the lender divides $25,000 by his $60,000 monthly income, resulting in a DTI of approximately 41.7%. This is near the upper limit for many jumbo programs but may still be acceptable with strong compensating factors.

Next, the lender evaluates Marcus's reserves. After his down payment and closing costs, he has $500,000 in liquid assets.

With a monthly housing payment of $15,000, this equates to over thirty-three months of reserves for the subject property alone. Additionally, the lender considers reserves for his existing properties, which further strengthens his profile.

Marcus's credit score is 740, reflecting strong financial management and low credit utilization. This high score enhances his application and may qualify him for better loan terms.

The lender also reviews the consistency of Marcus's deposits and confirms that they are derived from stable income sources, including rental income and business revenue. His diversified income streams provide additional confidence in his ability to sustain payments.

Despite the higher DTI, Marcus's strong reserves, low LTV, and excellent credit serve as powerful compensating factors. These strengths offset the risk associated with the large loan amount and investment property classification.

The lender approves Marcus for the jumbo bank statement mortgage loan, allowing him to acquire the luxury rental property. This purchase not only expands his portfolio but also positions him for increased cash flow and long-term appreciation.

This example illustrates how jumbo bank statement loans can be used to finance high-value investment properties. By balancing income, reserves, credit, and LTV, borrowers can navigate the complexities of investment property lending and achieve their financial goals.

Chapter 7

Jumbo Bank Statement Mortgage Loans for High-Value Properties

As you step into the highest tier of mortgage financing, jumbo bank statement loans for high-value properties represent the pinnacle of both opportunity and complexity. These loans are designed for borrowers seeking to finance luxury homes, estate-level properties, and premium real estate assets that often exceed standard jumbo thresholds. At this level, lending is no longer just about qualification—it is about precision, presentation, and positioning. Every detail of the borrower's financial profile is examined with heightened scrutiny, and every decision carries greater financial weight.

High-value properties are fundamentally different from standard real estate transactions. These homes often exist in competitive markets, feature unique architectural designs, and command prices that reflect exclusivity and desirability. For lenders, financing these properties involves a higher level of risk due to the size of the loan and the potential challenges associated with resale. As a result, borrowers must demonstrate not only strong financial capacity but also stability, consistency, and a well-structured financial profile. Jumbo bank statement loans provide a pathway for borrowers who have significant income that is not fully reflected on tax returns. This is especially common among entrepreneurs, business owners, and high-net-worth individuals who utilize strategic deductions and reinvestment strategies. By focusing on actual cash flow through bank statements, lenders gain a clearer picture of the borrower's true earning potential. However, at the high-value level, this flexibility is balanced by stricter requirements in other areas.

Loan size becomes one of the most defining factors in these transactions. As loan amounts increase beyond traditional jumbo levels, lenders often introduce additional overlays. These may include lower loan-to-value ratios, higher reserve requirements, stricter credit thresholds, and more detailed documentation. The goal is to mitigate risk while still providing access to financing for qualified borrowers.

Loan-to-value ratio is particularly important in high-value property financing. While standard jumbo loans may allow LTVs of up to 80%, high-value properties often require more conservative ratios, such as 70% to 75% or even lower. This means borrowers must be prepared to contribute significant down payments, often ranging from hundreds of thousands to millions of dollars. This equity not only reduces lender risk but also demonstrates the borrower's commitment to the transaction. Credit profile plays an even more critical role at this level. Lenders typically expect strong credit scores, often in the 720+ range, along with a history of responsible financial behavior. However, as with all jumbo bank statement loans, credit is evaluated holistically. A borrower with slightly lower credit may still qualify if they present exceptional strengths in other areas, such as reserves or income consistency.

Reserves become a cornerstone of approval for high-value properties. Lenders want to ensure that borrowers have the financial capacity to sustain large monthly payments over an extended period. Reserve requirements can range from twelve to twenty-four months or more, depending on the loan size and overall risk profile. These reserves must be liquid and verifiable, providing a clear safety net in the event of income fluctuations.

Income consistency is another critical factor. At higher loan amounts, lenders closely analyze deposit patterns to ensure that income is stable and recurring. Large fluctuations or irregular deposits can raise concerns, even if the overall income level is high. Borrowers must present a clean and consistent financial history that supports their ability to manage significant financial obligations.

Debt-to-income ratio is evaluated with precision. While some flexibility exists, lenders often prefer lower DTIs for high-value loans. This is because larger monthly payments require a greater margin of safety. A borrower with a DTI of 30% is generally viewed more favorably than one at 43%, even if both technically meet guidelines. Lower DTIs indicate a stronger ability to absorb financial changes and maintain stability.

Another important aspect of high-value property financing is property evaluation. Luxury homes often have unique features that can impact appraisal and marketability. Lenders assess not only the value of the property but also its appeal in the broader market. Properties that are highly customized or located in niche markets may present additional challenges. Understanding how property characteristics influence lender decisions is essential when selecting a high-value asset.

Liquidity is also a key consideration. Beyond reserves, lenders look at the borrower's overall asset profile, including investments, retirement accounts, and other financial holdings. A diversified asset base provides additional confidence and demonstrates long-term financial stability. Borrowers who can show substantial liquidity are often viewed more favorably, even if other aspects of their profile are slightly weaker.

Risk layering becomes especially significant at this level. Combining multiple risk factors—such as high LTV, lower credit, and limited reserves—can quickly lead to denial. However, strengthening one or more of these areas can offset risk and improve approval chances. This is where strategic planning becomes essential. Borrowers must understand how each element of their profile interacts and take steps to optimize their overall position.

Another critical factor is the borrower's financial narrative. At high loan amounts, lenders are not just evaluating numbers—they are evaluating the story behind those numbers. This includes understanding the borrower's business, income sources, and long-term financial trajectory. A clear and compelling narrative can make a significant difference in how the application is perceived.

Timing also plays a crucial role. Preparing for a high-value jumbo loan requires careful planning, often months or even years in advance. This includes maintaining consistent income, building reserves, optimizing credit, and structuring finances in a way that supports approval. Borrowers who take a proactive approach are far more likely to succeed.

One of the most powerful aspects of jumbo bank statement loans for high-value properties is the ability to leverage true income potential. These loans allow borrowers to access premium real estate opportunities that align with their financial capacity, even when traditional documentation falls short. This creates opportunities for lifestyle upgrades, wealth preservation, and long-term investment.

However, with these opportunities comes responsibility. High-value properties require disciplined financial management and a clear understanding of long-term obligations. Borrowers must be prepared to manage larger payments, maintain reserves, and adapt to changing financial conditions. Success in this space requires both confidence and caution.

As you move forward, it becomes clear that jumbo bank statement loans for high-value properties are about more than just financing—they are about strategy, preparation, and execution. By understanding how lenders evaluate these loans and positioning yourself accordingly, you can unlock access to some of the most desirable real estate opportunities available.

Real-Life Math Example: Financing a High-Value Property with a Jumbo Bank Statement Loan

Consider a borrower named Isabella, a successful entrepreneur who owns multiple businesses and is looking to purchase a luxury estate priced at $3,000,000. Isabella's tax returns show limited income due to deductions, but her bank statements reflect substantial cash flow. She decides to pursue a jumbo bank statement mortgage loan.

Isabella provides twenty-four months of business bank statements showing total deposits of $4,800,000. Dividing this by twenty-four months results in an average monthly income of $200,000. The lender applies a 35% expense factor, reducing her qualifying income to $130,000 per month.

Isabella plans to put down 30%, or $900,000, resulting in a loan amount of $2,100,000 and an LTV of 70%. This lower LTV aligns with lender requirements for high-value properties and significantly reduces risk.

Her estimated monthly housing payment, including taxes and insurance, is $20,000. She also has additional monthly debts totaling $5,000, bringing her total monthly obligations to $25,000.

To calculate her debt-to-income ratio, the lender divides $25,000 by her $130,000 monthly income, resulting in a DTI of approximately 19.2%. This low DTI is a strong indicator of her ability to manage the loan.

Next, the lender evaluates Isabella's reserves. After her down payment and closing costs, she has $600,000 in liquid assets.

With a monthly housing payment of $20,000, this equates to thirty months of reserves, far exceeding typical requirements.

Isabella's credit score is 750, with a strong history of on-time payments and low utilization. This high score further strengthens her application and may qualify her for favorable loan terms.

The lender also reviews the consistency of Isabella's deposits and confirms that they are derived from stable business income. Her diversified income streams provide additional confidence in her financial stability.

Despite the high loan amount, Isabella's strong income, low DTI, substantial reserves, and excellent credit create a low-risk profile. These factors work together as powerful compensating factors, offsetting the inherent risk of a large loan.

The lender approves Isabella for the jumbo bank statement mortgage loan, allowing her to purchase the luxury estate. This transaction demonstrates how high-value properties can be financed through strategic use of bank statement income and strong financial positioning.

This example highlights the importance of balancing all elements of the loan profile. By understanding how income, credit, reserves, and LTV interact, borrowers can successfully navigate the complexities of jumbo lending and achieve their goals in high-value real estate.

Chapter 8

Jumbo Bank Statement Mortgage Loan Refinancing and Cash-Out Strategies

As you move beyond acquisition and into the optimization phase of real estate ownership, refinancing becomes one of the most powerful financial tools available. Jumbo bank statement mortgage loans are not only designed to help borrowers purchase high-value properties—they also provide strategic pathways to restructure debt, improve cash flow, and unlock equity without relying on traditional income documentation. For self-employed borrowers and high-income individuals whose tax returns do not reflect their true earning power, these refinance strategies can be transformational.

Refinancing in the jumbo bank statement space operates differently from standard refinance transactions. Because these loans are already outside conforming guidelines, lenders take a more customized approach to evaluating risk. The borrower's current financial profile, property value, equity position, and income consistency all play a role in determining eligibility. Whether the goal is to lower a monthly payment, consolidate debt, or access cash for new investments, understanding how these factors interact is essential. One of the most common refinance strategies is the rate-and-term refinance. This involves replacing an existing loan with a new one that has better terms, such as a lower interest rate, a different loan term, or both. For borrowers with improved credit, stronger income, or increased property value, this can result in significant monthly savings and long-term interest reduction. In the jumbo bank statement context, this strategy allows borrowers to benefit from improved financial positioning without needing to rely on tax returns.

Another powerful strategy is the cash-out refinance. This allows borrowers to tap into the equity they have built in their property and convert it into liquid capital. For example, a borrower who purchased a property several years ago may have seen significant appreciation, combined with principal paydown. A cash-out refinance enables them to access that equity and use it for various purposes, such as investing in additional properties, funding business growth, consolidating high-interest debt, or building reserves.

Equity is the foundation of all refinance strategies. Lenders determine how much equity a borrower has by comparing the current market value of the property to the existing loan balance. This is expressed as the loan-to-value ratio. In jumbo refinance transactions, lenders typically require lower LTVs compared to purchases, especially for cash-out refinances. For example, while a purchase may allow 75% LTV, a cash-out refinance might be capped at 65% to 70%, depending on the borrower's profile and loan size.

Debt consolidation is another key benefit of refinancing. Many borrowers carry high-interest debt, such as credit cards or personal loans, which can significantly impact their financial stability. By using a cash-out refinance to pay off these obligations, borrowers can simplify their finances and potentially reduce their overall monthly payments. However, this strategy must be approached carefully, as it converts unsecured debt into secured debt tied to the property.

Liquidity is a central theme in jumbo refinance strategies. Having access to cash provides flexibility and security, especially for self-employed individuals. A cash-out refinance can create a financial buffer that allows borrowers to navigate fluctuations in income, seize investment opportunities, or handle unexpected expenses. Lenders view liquidity favorably, as it enhances the borrower's overall risk profile.

Income qualification remains a critical component of jumbo bank statement refinances. Just as with purchase loans, lenders analyze bank statements to determine qualifying income. Consistency, documentation, and the source of deposits are all evaluated. Borrowers must ensure that their financial activity reflects stable and recurring income, as this directly impacts approval.

Credit plays an important role in refinance transactions as well. Borrowers with improved credit scores may qualify for better interest rates and more favorable terms. Even small improvements in credit can result in significant savings over the life of a jumbo loan. This makes credit optimization an important step before initiating a refinance.

Another factor to consider is timing. Refinancing is most effective when market conditions align with the borrower's financial goals. This includes interest rate trends, property value appreciation, and the borrower's overall financial position. Acting at the right time can maximize the benefits of a refinance and minimize costs.

Costs are also an important consideration. Jumbo refinance transactions often involve closing costs, including appraisal fees, title insurance, and lender fees. Borrowers must evaluate whether the benefits of refinancing outweigh these costs. In many cases, the long-term savings or access to capital justifies the expense, but careful analysis is essential.

Appraisal plays a critical role in refinance transactions. The property's current value determines how much equity is available and influences the loan terms. High-value properties may require specialized appraisals, and ensuring that the property is presented in its best condition can impact the outcome.

Another important concept is the borrower's long-term strategy. Refinancing should align with broader financial goals, whether that involves reducing debt, expanding a real estate portfolio, or improving cash flow. Each decision should be made with a clear understanding of how it fits into the overall financial plan.

Risk management is also essential. While refinancing can provide significant benefits, it also introduces new obligations. Borrowers must ensure that they are not over-leveraging their property or taking on more debt than they can comfortably manage. Maintaining a balanced financial profile is key to long-term success.

One of the most powerful aspects of jumbo bank statement refinance strategies is their flexibility. These loans allow borrowers to adapt to changing financial circumstances and take control of their equity without being constrained by traditional income documentation. This flexibility creates opportunities that would otherwise be unavailable.

As you continue to build your understanding, it becomes clear that refinancing is not just a transaction—it is a strategic tool. By leveraging your property's equity, optimizing your loan terms, and aligning your financial profile with lender expectations, you can unlock new levels of financial potential.

Ultimately, jumbo bank statement mortgage loan refinancing and cash-out strategies provide a pathway to greater financial control, increased liquidity, and long-term wealth building. By mastering these concepts, you position yourself to make informed decisions and take advantage of opportunities that align with your goals.

Real-Life Math Example: Jumbo Cash-Out Refinance Strategy

Consider a borrower named David, a self-employed business owner who purchased a property five years ago for $1,800,000. Over time, the property has appreciated significantly and is now valued at $2,500,000. David's current loan balance is $1,200,000, and he is interested in accessing equity to invest in additional real estate.

First, the lender calculates David's current loan-to-value ratio by dividing his loan balance by the property value. $1,200,000 divided by $2,500,000 results in an LTV of 48%. This indicates that David has substantial equity in the property.

For a cash-out refinance, the lender allows a maximum LTV of 70%. This means David can borrow up to 70% of the property's value, which is $1,750,000. Subtracting his existing loan balance of $1,200,000 leaves $550,000 in available cash-out proceeds.

Next, the lender evaluates David's income using twelve months of bank statements. His total deposits equal $1,080,000, resulting in an average monthly income of $90,000. Because these are business accounts, the lender applies a 40% expense factor, reducing his qualifying income to $54,000 per month.

David's new loan amount of $1,750,000 results in a monthly housing payment of $14,500. He also has $3,500 in other monthly debts, bringing his total obligations to $18,000. Dividing $18,000 by $54,000 results in a DTI of approximately 33.3%, which is within acceptable limits for jumbo loans.

The lender then evaluates David's reserves. After the refinance, he plans to retain $200,000 in liquid assets. With a monthly housing payment of $14,500, this equates to nearly fourteen months of reserves, meeting the lender's requirement.

David's credit score is 735, with a strong payment history and low utilization. This enhances his profile and supports approval.

After reviewing all factors—equity, income, DTI, reserves, and credit—the lender approves David for the cash-out refinance. He receives $550,000 in cash, which he plans to use as down payments on additional investment properties. This strategy allows David to leverage his existing property to expand his portfolio and increase his income potential. By understanding how jumbo bank statement refinance calculations work, he is able to access capital and create new opportunities for growth.

This example demonstrates the power of refinancing as a financial tool. By strategically using equity, borrowers can unlock value, improve their financial position, and achieve their long-term goals in real estate.

Chapter 9

Jumbo Bank Statement Mortgage Loans with Low Credit or Financial Challenges

As you progress through the world of jumbo bank statement mortgage loans, one of the most important realities to understand is that not every borrower fits the "perfect" profile. While many discussions around jumbo lending focus on strong credit, large reserves, and flawless financial histories, the truth is that a significant number of borrowers fall somewhere in between. They may have experienced credit events, temporary financial setbacks, or inconsistencies in their financial profile. The key to success in these situations is not perfection—it is positioning, strategy, and the effective use of compensating factors.

Jumbo bank statement loans offer a unique opportunity for borrowers with non-traditional financial profiles, including those with lower credit scores or past credit challenges. Unlike conventional loans, which rely heavily on rigid guidelines and automated approvals, jumbo non-QM programs allow for a more flexible, case-by-case evaluation. This flexibility creates pathways for borrowers who might otherwise be denied, but it also requires a deeper understanding of how lenders assess risk. Credit challenges can take many forms. These may include late payments, collections, charge-offs, high credit utilization, or major events such as bankruptcies, foreclosures, or short sales. Each of these factors impacts the borrower's risk profile, but they do not automatically disqualify a borrower from obtaining a jumbo bank statement loan. Instead, lenders evaluate the severity, timing, and context of these events.

One of the most important concepts in this space is seasoning. Seasoning refers to the amount of time that has passed since a negative credit event occurred. Lenders place significant weight on how recent an event is, as well as the borrower's behavior since that event. For example, a bankruptcy that occurred five years ago with a strong payment history afterward may be viewed more favorably than a recent late payment. Demonstrating a pattern of recovery and responsible financial behavior is critical.

Another key factor is credit trajectory. Lenders are not just looking at where your credit stands today—they are also evaluating the direction it is moving. An improving credit profile signals positive financial habits and reduces perceived risk. Borrowers who actively work to pay down debt, reduce utilization, and maintain on-time payments can significantly strengthen their application, even if their current score is not ideal. Debt management plays a central role in overcoming credit challenges. High levels of debt relative to income can increase risk, particularly in jumbo lending. By reducing outstanding balances and simplifying debt structures, borrowers can improve both their credit profile and their debt-to-income ratio. This dual benefit makes debt reduction one of the most effective strategies for strengthening an application.

Compensating factors become especially important for borrowers with credit challenges. These are the strengths within the borrower's profile that offset weaknesses and provide reassurance to the lender. Strong reserves, a lower loan-to-value ratio, consistent income, and a stable financial history can all serve as powerful compensating factors. For example, a borrower with a lower credit score but significant liquidity and a large down payment may still be approved because the overall risk is balanced.

Loan-to-value ratio is one of the most effective tools for mitigating risk. Borrowers with credit challenges may be required to put down larger amounts, often 25% to 35% or more, depending on the severity of their profile. This increased equity reduces the lender's exposure and demonstrates the borrower's commitment to the transaction. It also creates a buffer that protects both the borrower and the lender in the event of market fluctuations. Reserves are equally critical. For borrowers with lower credit, lenders often require higher levels of reserves to ensure that the borrower can sustain payments even during periods of financial stress. These reserves provide a safety net and serve as a strong indicator of financial stability. In many cases, increasing reserves can make the difference between approval and denial.

Income consistency is another key factor. Even when credit is less than ideal, a borrower with stable and predictable income can present a compelling case. Bank statement loans allow lenders to evaluate actual cash flow, which can work in the borrower's favor if their deposits reflect consistent earnings. This is particularly beneficial for self-employed individuals who may have strong income despite credit challenges.

Another important consideration is the explanation of credit events. Lenders often require a written explanation detailing the circumstances behind negative credit items. Providing a clear, honest, and well-documented explanation can help underwriters understand the context and assess the borrower's current risk more accurately. Life events such as medical issues, business disruptions, or economic downturns may be viewed more favorably when properly explained.

Risk layering is especially critical in this context. Combining multiple risk factors—such as low credit, high LTV, and limited reserves—can significantly reduce the likelihood of approval. However, strengthening one or more of these areas can offset risk. For example, increasing the down payment and reserves can compensate for a lower credit score, creating a more balanced profile.

Lender overlays also play a significant role. Some lenders are more flexible than others when it comes to credit challenges. This means that finding the right lender is often just as important as improving your financial profile. Borrowers who understand the landscape and work with knowledgeable professionals can identify lenders whose guidelines align with their situation.

Timing is another critical factor. Borrowers with recent credit events may benefit from waiting until additional seasoning has occurred. Even a few months of improved credit behavior can make a significant difference in how the application is evaluated. Strategic timing allows borrowers to present a stronger and more stable profile.

Another key aspect is financial discipline. Borrowers must demonstrate that they have learned from past challenges and are now managing their finances responsibly. This includes maintaining consistent deposits, avoiding new debt, and building reserves. These actions not only improve the borrower's profile but also reinforce confidence in their ability to manage a jumbo loan. Ultimately, jumbo bank statement mortgage loans for borrowers with credit challenges are about transformation. They provide an opportunity to move forward, rebuild financial strength, and access opportunities that might otherwise seem out of reach. By understanding how lenders evaluate risk and taking proactive steps to strengthen your profile, you can position yourself for success even in the face of past challenges.

Real-Life Math Example: Overcoming Credit Challenges in a Jumbo Loan Scenario

Consider a borrower named Carlos, a self-employed contractor who is looking to purchase a home priced at $1,400,000. Carlos has strong income but experienced financial difficulties three years ago, resulting in several late payments and a temporary drop in his credit score.

Carlos provides twelve months of bank statements showing total deposits of $840,000, resulting in an average monthly income of $70,000. Because these are business accounts, the lender applies a 45% expense factor, reducing his qualifying income to $38,500 per month.

Carlos plans to put down 20%, or $280,000, resulting in a loan amount of $1,120,000 and an LTV of 80%. His estimated monthly housing payment is $11,000, and he has additional debts totaling $3,000 per month. This brings his total monthly obligations to $14,000.

Dividing $14,000 by his $38,500 monthly income results in a DTI of approximately 36.4%, which is within acceptable limits. However, Carlos's credit score is 660, which presents a challenge for jumbo lending.

To improve his profile, Carlos takes several strategic steps. First, he increases his down payment to 30%, or $420,000, reducing his loan amount to $980,000 and lowering his LTV to 70%. This significantly reduces lender risk.

Next, Carlos focuses on building reserves. After his down payment and closing costs, he ensures that he has $150,000 in liquid assets. With a monthly housing payment of $11,000, this equates to over thirteen months of reserves, exceeding lender requirements.

Carlos also works on improving his credit by paying down outstanding balances and maintaining on-time payments. Over several months, his credit score increases to 690, moving him closer to the lender's preferred range.

Additionally, Carlos provides a detailed letter explaining the circumstances behind his past credit issues, including documentation showing that his financial situation has stabilized. This helps the lender understand the context and view his current profile more favorably.

With these adjustments, Carlos's application now includes strong compensating factors: a lower LTV, substantial reserves, improving credit, and consistent income. These elements offset the initial credit challenges and create a balanced risk profile.

The lender reviews the application and determines that, despite the lower credit score, Carlos presents a manageable level of risk. His financial improvements and strong compensating factors provide confidence in his ability to repay the loan.

Carlos is approved for the jumbo bank statement mortgage loan and successfully purchases his home. This outcome demonstrates that credit challenges do not have to be a barrier to success. With the right strategy and preparation, borrowers can overcome obstacles and achieve their real estate goals.

This example highlights the importance of understanding how to navigate credit challenges in jumbo lending. By focusing on what can be controlled—such as reserves, LTV, and income consistency—borrowers can create opportunities even in less-than-perfect situations.

Chapter 10

Advanced Jumbo Bank Statement Mortgage Loan Structuring Strategies

As you reach the final stage of mastering jumbo bank statement mortgage loans, it becomes clear that success is no longer about simply qualifying—it is about engineering approvals with precision. Advanced structuring is where experienced borrowers separate themselves from the average applicant. It involves strategically aligning income, assets, credit, timing, and property selection to create a loan profile that not only meets guidelines but optimizes outcomes. At this level, every detail matters, and even small adjustments can significantly impact approval, loan terms, and long-term financial success.

Advanced structuring begins with a deep understanding of how lenders evaluate risk holistically. Rather than focusing on individual metrics in isolation, lenders assess how all components of a borrower's profile interact. This includes income derived from bank statements, loan-to-value ratio, debt-to-income ratio, reserves, credit, and property characteristics. The goal is to create a balanced profile where strengths offset weaknesses and risk is minimized across all areas. One of the most powerful tools in advanced structuring is income optimization. This involves analyzing bank statement deposits and determining the most favorable way to present income. Borrowers may choose between personal and business bank statements, depending on which produces higher qualifying income. In some cases, combining both can yield the best results. Additionally, leveraging CPA-prepared profit and loss statements to reduce expense factors can significantly increase qualifying income and improve DTI.

Timing deposits is another advanced strategy. Because lenders average deposits over a specific period, ensuring consistent and predictable income during that timeframe is critical. Borrowers who anticipate applying for a loan can structure their financial activity in advance, smoothing out irregularities and avoiding large unexplained transactions. This proactive approach creates a cleaner and more stable financial profile.

Another key strategy is managing loan-to-value ratio. While meeting minimum LTV requirements is necessary, optimizing LTV can unlock better loan terms and reduce risk. Increasing the down payment—even slightly—can improve approval chances, lower interest rates, and reduce reserve requirements. Advanced borrowers often evaluate multiple scenarios to determine the optimal balance between cash investment and loan size. Debt-to-income ratio can also be strategically managed. This may involve paying down existing debts, restructuring obligations, or timing the payoff of certain liabilities before applying. Reducing monthly obligations directly improves DTI, which is a critical factor in jumbo lending. In some cases, eliminating a single large debt can make the difference between approval and denial.

Reserves can be structured strategically as well. Borrowers may consolidate assets, move funds into more liquid accounts, or delay certain investments to ensure that reserve requirements are met or exceeded. Strong reserves not only satisfy lender requirements but also act as a powerful compensating factor that can offset other risks.

Credit optimization is another essential component. Even small improvements in credit score can have a significant impact on loan terms, particularly for jumbo loans. Borrowers can improve their credit by reducing utilization, correcting errors, and maintaining consistent payment behavior. Advanced structuring involves timing these improvements so that they are reflected in the credit report at the time of application.

Another advanced concept is layering income sources. Borrowers with multiple streams of income—such as business revenue, rental income, and investment distributions—can combine these sources to strengthen their overall profile.

However, each source must be documented and presented clearly to avoid confusion during underwriting. Proper organization and documentation are critical when using this strategy.

Property selection also plays a strategic role. Choosing a property that aligns with lender preferences can simplify the approval process. Properties in strong markets with high demand are viewed more favorably, while unique or highly specialized properties may require additional scrutiny. Advanced borrowers consider not only the property's value but also its marketability and alignment with lender guidelines.

Another powerful strategy is leveraging multiple lenders. Because jumbo loans are subject to lender-specific overlays, different lenders may offer different solutions for the same borrower. Advanced structuring involves identifying lenders whose guidelines align with the borrower's profile and exploring multiple options to find the best fit.

Risk layering must be carefully managed. Combining multiple risk factors—such as high LTV, lower credit, and limited reserves—can create challenges. Advanced structuring involves identifying these risks and taking steps to mitigate them. This may include increasing the down payment, improving credit, or strengthening reserves to create a more balanced profile.

Another key element is scenario analysis. Advanced borrowers often evaluate multiple loan scenarios before applying. This includes adjusting variables such as down payment, loan amount, and income structure to determine the most favorable outcome. By comparing different options, borrowers can make informed decisions that optimize both approval and long-term financial performance.

Liquidity management is also critical. Maintaining access to cash while meeting lender requirements requires careful planning. Borrowers must balance the need for reserves with the desire to invest or deploy capital elsewhere. Advanced structuring involves creating a financial plan that supports both immediate loan approval and long-term financial goals.

Communication and presentation are equally important. At higher loan amounts, underwriters often rely on the clarity and organization of the borrower's file. Providing well-documented income, clear explanations of financial activity, and a cohesive narrative can significantly improve the likelihood of approval. Advanced structuring is not just about numbers—it is about how those numbers are presented.

Another advanced strategy is preparing for future scalability. Borrowers who plan to acquire additional properties or refinance in the future must structure their finances in a way that supports ongoing growth. This includes maintaining consistent income, preserving reserves, and avoiding over-leveraging. A well-structured profile today can create opportunities for future transactions.

Ultimately, advanced jumbo bank statement loan structuring is about control. It allows borrowers to take ownership of their financial profile and shape it in a way that aligns with lender expectations. By understanding the nuances of underwriting and applying strategic planning, borrowers can move beyond basic qualification and achieve optimal outcomes.

This chapter represents the culmination of everything you have learned throughout this series. By integrating these advanced strategies, you gain the ability to navigate even the most complex jumbo lending scenarios with confidence and precision.

Real-Life Math Example: Advanced Structuring for Optimal Approval

Consider a borrower named Sophia, a high-income entrepreneur seeking to purchase a property priced at $2,400,000. Sophia has strong income but needs to optimize her profile to secure the best possible loan terms.

Sophia provides twelve months of business bank statements showing total deposits of $1,440,000, resulting in an average monthly income of $120,000. The lender initially applies a 50% expense factor, reducing her qualifying income to $60,000 per month.

Sophia works with her CPA to provide a profit and loss statement showing that her actual expenses are closer to 30%. The lender agrees to use this lower expense ratio, increasing her qualifying income to $84,000 per month.

Her initial plan is to put down 20%, or $480,000, resulting in a loan amount of $1,920,000 and an LTV of 80%. Her estimated monthly housing payment is $16,000, and she has additional debts of $4,000 per month, bringing her total obligations to $20,000.

Dividing $20,000 by her initial qualifying income of $60,000 results in a DTI of 33.3%. However, with the adjusted income of $84,000, her DTI drops to approximately 23.8%, significantly improving her profile.

Sophia then evaluates her reserves. After her down payment and closing costs, she initially has $120,000 in liquid assets, which equates to 7.5 months of reserves. To strengthen her application, she reallocates funds from an investment account, increasing her reserves to $250,000, or over fifteen months.

Next, Sophia decides to increase her down payment to 25%, or

$600,000, reducing her loan amount to $1,800,000 and lowering her LTV to 75%. This adjustment further reduces risk and improves her chances of approval.

Sophia also pays down $50,000 in credit card balances, reducing her utilization and increasing her credit score from 700 to 730. This improvement positions her for better loan terms and enhances her overall profile.

With these adjustments, Sophia's application now includes higher qualifying income, lower DTI, stronger reserves, improved credit, and a lower LTV. Each of these elements works together to create a balanced and low-risk profile.

The lender reviews her application and determines that she meets all requirements with strong compensating factors. As a result, she is approved for the jumbo bank statement mortgage loan with favorable terms.

This example demonstrates how advanced structuring can transform a loan scenario. By strategically adjusting income, reserves, credit, and LTV, Sophia is able to optimize her profile and achieve a superior outcome.

It highlights the importance of proactive planning, attention to detail, and a deep understanding of how lenders evaluate risk. With the right approach, borrowers can take control of the process and unlock the full potential of jumbo bank statement lending.

Chapter 11

Building a Repeatable Jumbo Bank Statement Loan System for Long-Term Wealth

By the time you reach this stage, the conversation is no longer just about qualifying for a single loan. It is about building a system—a repeatable, scalable strategy that allows you to continuously leverage jumbo bank statement mortgage loans to grow wealth, expand your real estate footprint, and create long-term financial security. The most successful borrowers do not approach each transaction as an isolated event. Instead, they think in terms of cycles, systems, and long-term positioning.

A repeatable system begins with clarity. You must understand your financial profile, your income structure, your risk tolerance, and your long-term goals. Whether your objective is to build a portfolio of high-value rental properties, upgrade your primary residence over time, or create a hybrid strategy that combines lifestyle and investment, every decision should align with a larger plan. Without this clarity, it becomes easy to overextend, misallocate capital, or miss opportunities.

The foundation of this system is consistency. Jumbo bank statement loans rely heavily on deposit history, credit behavior, and financial stability. This means that your day-to-day financial habits directly impact your ability to qualify for future loans. Maintaining consistent deposits, avoiding unnecessary financial volatility, and preserving a clean financial record are essential. Think of your bank statements as a long-term asset—they tell the story that lenders will evaluate again and again.

Income scalability is a central component of this system. As your income grows, your borrowing capacity increases. However, growth must be structured properly. Expanding your business, diversifying income streams, and maintaining consistent cash flow all contribute to a stronger financial profile. The goal is not just to increase income, but to present it in a way that is clear, stable, and favorable for underwriting.

Another key element is equity management. Each property you acquire or refinance becomes a building block in your overall system. As property values appreciate and loan balances decrease, equity accumulates. This equity can be leveraged through refinancing or cash-out strategies to fund future acquisitions. Understanding how to manage and deploy equity effectively is one of the most powerful tools in long-term wealth building.

Liquidity must also be carefully managed. While it is important to invest capital into properties, maintaining sufficient reserves is critical for both loan approvals and financial stability. A strong liquidity position not only satisfies lender requirements but also provides flexibility to navigate market changes and seize new opportunities. The balance between investing and preserving liquidity is a key aspect of advanced financial strategy.

Credit management remains an ongoing priority. Your credit profile is not a one-time consideration—it is a continuous factor that influences every loan you pursue. Maintaining low utilization, making timely payments, and avoiding unnecessary credit inquiries all contribute to a strong and stable credit profile. Over time, this consistency can lead to better loan terms and increased borrowing capacity.

Portfolio diversification is another important concept. While real estate is a powerful wealth-building tool, relying on a single type of property or market can increase risk. Diversifying across property types, locations, and income strategies can create a more resilient portfolio. For example, combining primary residences, long-term rentals, and short-term rental properties can provide multiple streams of income and reduce exposure to market fluctuations.

Another critical component of a repeatable system is timing. Understanding when to acquire, refinance, or hold properties is essential. Market conditions, interest rates, and property values all influence these decisions. Successful borrowers monitor these factors and act strategically, rather than reactively. Timing is not about predicting the market perfectly—it is about recognizing opportunities and being prepared to act when they arise.

Leverage is at the heart of this system. Jumbo bank statement loans allow you to control high-value assets with a relatively smaller amount of capital. When used responsibly, leverage can amplify returns and accelerate wealth creation. However, it must be managed carefully. Over-leveraging can increase risk and reduce flexibility, especially during market downturns. The key is to use leverage strategically, ensuring that each transaction strengthens your overall position.

Another advanced concept is the use of layering strategies. This involves combining different loan types, income sources, and financial tools to achieve optimal results. For example, a borrower may use a jumbo bank statement loan for one property while utilizing a DSCR loan for another. By understanding the strengths and limitations of each option, you can create a more flexible and effective financing strategy.

Documentation and organization are essential for scalability. As your portfolio grows, so does the complexity of your financial profile. Keeping detailed records of income, expenses, assets, and liabilities ensures that you can quickly and efficiently present your information to lenders. This not only speeds up the approval process but also reduces the likelihood of errors or delays.

Another important aspect is building relationships. Working with experienced lenders, brokers, and financial professionals can provide valuable insights and access to opportunities. These relationships can help you navigate complex scenarios, identify favorable programs, and streamline the loan process. Over time, having a trusted network can become a significant advantage.

Risk management is an ongoing responsibility. Every transaction introduces new variables, and maintaining a balanced portfolio requires continuous evaluation. This includes monitoring cash flow, maintaining reserves, and adjusting strategies as needed. The goal is to create a system that is both growth-oriented and resilient.

Mindset plays a crucial role in building a repeatable system. Success in jumbo lending requires discipline, patience, and a long-term perspective. It is not about chasing quick wins—it is about making strategic decisions that compound over time. By staying focused on your goals and maintaining consistent financial habits, you can create a system that supports sustained growth.

Ultimately, building a repeatable jumbo bank statement loan system is about creating a framework that allows you to continuously leverage your financial profile to achieve greater outcomes. It is about turning knowledge into action, strategy into results, and opportunities into long-term wealth.

Real-Life Math Example: Building a Scalable Jumbo Loan Strategy

Consider a borrower named Elena, a self-employed entrepreneur who is focused on building a portfolio of high-value properties over the next ten years. Elena starts with a strong income profile and wants to create a repeatable system using jumbo bank statement loans.

Elena's current annual deposits total $1,200,000, resulting in an average monthly income of $100,000. Using a 40% expense factor, her qualifying income is $60,000 per month. She begins by purchasing her first property for $1,500,000, putting down 25%, or $375,000, resulting in a loan amount of $1,125,000.

Her monthly housing payment is $11,000, and she has no additional debt. Her DTI is calculated as $11,000 divided by $60,000, resulting in 18.3%. This low DTI positions her well for approval.

Over the next three years, the property appreciates to $1,900,000, and her loan balance decreases to $1,050,000. Her equity has increased significantly. She decides to perform a cash-out refinance at 70% LTV, allowing her to borrow up to $1,330,000. Subtracting her existing loan balance, she accesses $280,000 in cash.

Elena uses this cash as a down payment on a second property priced at $1,600,000, again putting down approximately 25%. Her income has also grown during this time, with annual deposits increasing to $1,500,000, resulting in a monthly income of $125,000. After applying a 40% expense factor, her qualifying income is $75,000 per month.

Her combined monthly obligations for both properties total $20,000. Dividing $20,000 by $75,000 results in a DTI of 26.7%, which remains within acceptable limits.

Elena continues this process, using appreciation, income growth, and strategic refinancing to acquire additional properties. Each transaction builds on the previous one, creating a compounding effect. By maintaining strong reserves, consistent income, and a balanced portfolio, she is able to scale her investments without overextending.

After ten years, Elena owns multiple high-value properties with significant equity and strong cash flow. Her disciplined approach to structuring income, managing leverage, and reinvesting capital allows her to build substantial wealth.

This example demonstrates how a repeatable system can transform individual transactions into a long-term strategy. By understanding the mechanics of jumbo bank statement loans and applying them consistently, borrowers can create a scalable framework for financial growth and success.

Chapter 12

The Long-Term Exit Strategy and Wealth Optimization with Jumbo Bank Statement Loans

As you reach the final chapter of this series, the focus shifts from acquisition and growth to optimization and exit. Building a portfolio using jumbo bank statement mortgage loans is a powerful strategy, but true financial success is defined by how well you manage, protect, and eventually transition that wealth. An exit strategy is not something you think about at the end—it is something you design from the beginning and refine over time. It ensures that your efforts translate into long-term financial freedom, stability, and legacy.

The concept of an exit strategy in real estate goes beyond simply selling properties. It involves understanding when to hold, when to refinance, when to liquidate, and how to structure your assets to achieve maximum efficiency. Each decision is influenced by market conditions, personal goals, tax considerations, and financial positioning. Jumbo bank statement loans provide flexibility throughout this process, allowing borrowers to adapt and optimize without being constrained by traditional income documentation. One of the most common exit strategies is appreciation-based selling. Over time, high-value properties often increase in value, particularly in strong markets. By holding a property through periods of appreciation, borrowers can build substantial equity. When the time is right, selling the property allows them to realize those gains. However, timing is critical. Selling too early may limit potential returns, while holding too long may expose the property to market downturns.

Another strategy is cash flow optimization. Instead of selling, borrowers may choose to hold properties and maximize rental income. This is particularly relevant for investment properties financed through jumbo bank statement loans. By increasing rents, reducing expenses, or improving property management, borrowers can enhance cash flow and create a steady income stream. This approach focuses on long-term income rather than immediate capital gains.

Refinancing plays a central role in wealth optimization. As properties appreciate and loan balances decrease, borrowers can access equity through cash-out refinances. This allows them to reinvest capital, pay down other debts, or improve liquidity. Refinancing can also be used to adjust loan terms, reduce interest rates, or transition into more favorable financial positions. In many cases, refinancing becomes a key component of both growth and exit strategies. Debt management is another critical aspect. While leverage is a powerful tool for growth, reducing debt over time can enhance financial stability and increase net worth. Some borrowers choose to pay down loans aggressively, while others maintain leverage to maximize returns. The optimal approach depends on individual goals, risk tolerance, and market conditions.

Tax considerations are an essential part of any exit strategy. Real estate transactions can have significant tax implications, including capital gains taxes and depreciation recapture. Strategies such as 1031 exchanges can allow borrowers to defer taxes by reinvesting proceeds into new properties. Understanding these options and planning accordingly can significantly impact overall returns.

Portfolio restructuring is another advanced strategy. As your portfolio grows, it may become necessary to adjust your holdings to align with changing goals or market conditions. This could involve selling underperforming properties, consolidating assets, or shifting focus to different property types or locations. Regular evaluation ensures that your portfolio remains optimized for both performance and risk.

Liquidity planning is also crucial. While real estate is a valuable asset, it is not always easily accessible. Ensuring that you have sufficient liquid assets allows you to navigate unexpected expenses, seize opportunities, and maintain financial flexibility. Balancing real estate investments with liquid assets is a key component of long-term stability.

Another important consideration is lifestyle alignment. As your financial situation evolves, your priorities may change. Your exit strategy should reflect not only financial goals but also personal aspirations. Whether it involves upgrading your primary residence, reducing your workload, or transitioning into retirement, your strategy should support the life you want to create.

Risk management remains a constant throughout the exit process. Market conditions can change, and properties that once performed well may face new challenges. Monitoring your portfolio, maintaining reserves, and staying informed about market trends helps mitigate risk and protect your investments.

Legacy planning is another dimension of long-term strategy. For many borrowers, real estate is not just about personal wealth—it is about creating opportunities for future generations. Structuring your assets in a way that facilitates inheritance, minimizes taxes, and ensures continuity can have a lasting impact.

Another advanced concept is phased exits. Instead of selling all properties at once, borrowers may choose to exit gradually. This allows them to manage tax implications, maintain income streams, and adapt to changing conditions. Phased strategies provide flexibility and reduce the risk associated with large, single transactions.

Market awareness is essential when planning an exit. Understanding trends in property values, interest rates, and demand allows you to make informed decisions about timing. Successful exits are often the result of careful observation and strategic action rather than reactive decisions.

One of the most powerful aspects of jumbo bank statement loans is their ability to support multiple stages of the real estate lifecycle. From acquisition to growth to exit, these loans provide flexibility and adaptability. By leveraging this flexibility, borrowers can create strategies that evolve with their financial situation.

As you reflect on the journey through this series, it becomes clear that success in jumbo bank statement lending is not defined by a single transaction. It is defined by the ability to build, manage, and optimize a portfolio over time. Each chapter has provided tools and insights that contribute to this larger objective.

Ultimately, the goal of an exit strategy is not just to maximize financial returns—it is to create a system that supports long-term freedom, security, and fulfillment. By planning ahead, making informed decisions, and staying aligned with your goals, you can ensure that your efforts result in meaningful and lasting outcomes.

Real-Life Math Example: Long-Term Exit and Wealth Optimization Strategy

Consider a borrower named Victor, who has built a portfolio of three high-value properties over ten years using jumbo bank statement mortgage loans. His goal is to optimize his wealth and transition into a more passive income-focused strategy.

Victor's portfolio includes three properties valued at $1,800,000, $2,200,000, and $2,500,000, for a total value of $6,500,000. His combined loan balances total $3,200,000, giving him $3,300,000 in equity.

Victor evaluates his options. He could sell all properties and realize his equity, but this would result in significant capital gains taxes. Instead, he considers a phased approach.

First, Victor decides to sell one property valued at $2,200,000 with a loan balance of $1,000,000. After paying off the loan, he realizes $1,200,000 in proceeds. He uses a 1031 exchange to reinvest this amount into a new property, deferring taxes and maintaining his investment position. Next, Victor performs a cash-out refinance on his $2,500,000 property. At a 70% LTV, he can borrow $1,750,000. With an existing loan balance of $1,200,000, he accesses $550,000 in cash. He uses this cash to pay down debt on his remaining property, reducing his overall leverage.

Victor also focuses on cash flow optimization. By increasing rents and improving property management, he raises his monthly rental income from $18,000 to $24,000 across his portfolio. His total monthly mortgage payments are $15,000, resulting in a net cash flow of $9,000 per month.

Over time, Victor continues to evaluate his portfolio. As property values increase and loans are paid down, his equity grows. He gradually reduces debt while maintaining strong cash flow, creating a balanced and stable financial position.

By the end of his strategy, Victor has optimized his portfolio to generate consistent income while preserving equity. His phased approach allows him to manage taxes, maintain liquidity, and adapt to changing conditions.

This example demonstrates how an effective exit strategy can transform a portfolio into a long-term wealth engine. By combining selling, refinancing, and cash flow optimization, Victor achieves both financial stability and growth. It highlights the importance of planning, flexibility, and strategic decision-making. With the right approach, borrowers can transition from active growth to sustainable wealth, ensuring that their efforts result in lasting success.

Chapter 13

Mastering the Jumbo Bank Statement Loan Process from Application to Closing

As you bring together everything you've learned throughout this series, the final piece of mastery lies in execution. Understanding guidelines, structuring income, optimizing credit, and building reserves are all critical—but none of it matters if you cannot successfully navigate the loan process from application to closing. This chapter is about precision, preparation, and control. It is about knowing exactly what happens at each stage, anticipating challenges before they arise, and positioning yourself to move through the process smoothly and successfully.

The jumbo bank statement loan process begins long before you submit an application. Preparation is the foundation. This includes organizing your bank statements, ensuring consistency in deposits, reviewing your credit profile, and verifying your available assets. At the jumbo level, lenders expect a high degree of organization. Your financial documents must tell a clear, consistent story that aligns with your application. Any discrepancies or inconsistencies can lead to delays, additional conditions, or even denial.

The initial stage of the process is pre-qualification or pre-approval. This is where the lender evaluates your financial profile at a high level to determine your eligibility. During this stage, you will provide basic documentation, including bank statements, asset statements, and credit authorization. The goal is to establish a preliminary understanding of your borrowing capacity and identify any potential issues early on.

Pre-approval is particularly important in jumbo lending, as it strengthens your position when making an offer on a property. Sellers of high-value properties often expect buyers to demonstrate financial capability upfront. A strong pre-approval not only gives you confidence but also signals to sellers that you are a serious and qualified buyer.

Once you move into the formal application stage, the process becomes more detailed. You will submit a complete set of documentation, including bank statements, identification, asset verification, and any additional information required by the lender. At this stage, accuracy is critical. Every number, date, and detail must align. Inconsistencies can trigger additional scrutiny and slow down the process.

The file then moves into processing, where the lender reviews your documentation and prepares it for underwriting. The processor acts as a bridge between you and the underwriter, ensuring that all required documents are collected and organized. This stage often involves requests for additional information, known as conditions. Responding to these requests quickly and thoroughly is essential for maintaining momentum.

Underwriting is the most critical stage of the process. This is where the lender conducts a detailed evaluation of your financial profile, income, assets, credit, and property. In jumbo bank statement loans, underwriting is often manual, meaning that underwriters apply judgment and experience rather than relying solely on automated systems. This makes the quality of your file and the clarity of your financial story even more important.

During underwriting, the lender will analyze your bank statements to calculate qualifying income. They will review deposit patterns, identify recurring income, and exclude non-qualifying deposits. They will also evaluate your debt-to-income ratio, loan-to-value ratio, reserves, and credit profile. Each of these factors contributes to the overall risk assessment.

Conditions are a normal part of underwriting. These are requests for additional documentation or clarification.

Common conditions may include explanations for large deposits, verification of income sources, or updated asset statements. While conditions can feel overwhelming, they are simply part of the process. The key is to address them promptly and provide clear, complete responses.

Appraisal is another critical component. The lender will order an appraisal to determine the property's value and ensure it supports the loan amount. For high-value properties, appraisals may be more complex and require additional analysis. Ensuring that the property is well-presented and that comparable sales support the value can help avoid issues.

Once underwriting is satisfied and all conditions are cleared, the file moves to final approval. This means that the lender has determined that you meet all requirements and is ready to proceed to closing. However, final approval is not the end of the process. There are still steps that must be completed before the loan is funded.

The closing stage involves signing the final loan documents and completing the transaction. This includes reviewing the closing disclosure, which outlines the final terms of the loan, including interest rate, monthly payment, and closing costs. It is important to review this document carefully to ensure that everything matches your expectations. Funding is the final step. Once all documents are signed and any remaining conditions are met, the lender releases the funds, and the transaction is complete. At this point, ownership is transferred, and the loan is officially in place.

One of the most important aspects of mastering this process is communication. Staying in regular contact with your lender, responding quickly to requests, and asking questions when needed can significantly improve the experience. Clear communication helps prevent misunderstandings and keeps the process moving forward.

Another key factor is timing. Jumbo loans often take longer than conventional loans due to their complexity. Planning ahead and allowing sufficient time for each stage can help avoid unnecessary stress. Being proactive and prepared ensures that you are not rushing to meet deadlines.

Organization is your greatest asset throughout this process. Keeping all documents in one place, maintaining clear records, and ensuring that everything is up to date can make a significant difference. A well-organized file not only speeds up the process but also creates confidence for the lender.

Another important consideration is avoiding financial changes during the process. Large purchases, new debt, or significant changes in income can impact your approval. Maintaining stability from application to closing is essential. Lenders expect consistency, and any changes can trigger additional review.

Ultimately, mastering the jumbo bank statement loan process is about control. It is about understanding each step, preparing thoroughly, and executing with precision. By doing so, you can navigate even the most complex transactions with confidence and achieve successful outcomes.

Real-Life Math Example: Navigating the Loan Process Step by Step

Consider a borrower named Daniel, who is applying for a jumbo bank statement mortgage loan to purchase a property priced at $1,900,000. Daniel has prepared his financial profile and is ready to move through the loan process.

During pre-approval, Daniel provides twelve months of bank statements showing total deposits of $1,200,000, resulting in an average monthly income of $100,000. The lender applies a 40% expense factor, reducing his qualifying income to $60,000 per month. Based on this income, Daniel is pre-approved for a loan amount of $1,425,000 with a 25% down payment.

As Daniel moves into the application stage, he submits all required documentation, including asset statements showing

$400,000 in liquid assets. His estimated monthly housing payment is $14,000, and he has $4,000 in additional monthly debt, resulting in total obligations of $18,000. Dividing $18,000 by $60,000 results in a DTI of 30%, which meets lender requirements.

During processing, the lender identifies a large deposit of $50,000 in Daniel's bank statements. The processor requests an explanation and documentation. Daniel provides a contract showing that the deposit was a client payment, which satisfies the condition.

In underwriting, the lender reviews Daniel's full profile. His loan-to-value ratio is 75%, his reserves are approximately fifteen months based on his remaining assets, and his credit score is 720. These factors create a strong overall profile.

The appraisal comes in at $1,920,000, slightly above the purchase price, supporting the loan amount. This eliminates any concerns about property value.

The underwriter issues a conditional approval, requesting updated bank statements and verification of Daniel's business activity. Daniel provides the requested documents promptly, and the conditions are cleared.

Daniel receives final approval and moves to closing. The

closing disclosure shows a monthly payment of $14,200, slightly higher than the initial estimate due to updated tax calculations. Daniel reviews and accepts the terms. At closing, Daniel signs the final documents, and the lender funds the loan. The transaction is completed successfully, and Daniel becomes the owner of the property.

This example demonstrates how each stage of the loan process works in practice. By preparing thoroughly, responding to conditions quickly, and maintaining a stable financial profile, Daniel is able to navigate the process smoothly and achieve approval.

It highlights the importance of understanding not just the numbers, but the process itself. With the right preparation and execution, borrowers can move from application to closing with confidence and success.

Chapter 14

Avoiding Mistakes and Maximizing Approval Success in Jumbo Bank Statement Loans

As you approach mastery in jumbo bank statement mortgage lending, one of the most valuable skills you can develop is the ability to avoid costly mistakes. At higher loan amounts, even small errors can lead to delays, additional conditions, or outright denial. Unlike conventional loans, jumbo bank statement loans rely heavily on interpretation, documentation, and risk assessment. This means that your financial profile must not only be strong—it must be presented correctly, consistently, and strategically.

One of the most common mistakes borrowers make is underestimating the importance of clean bank statements. Because income is derived from deposits, every transaction is subject to review. Large, unexplained deposits, frequent transfers between accounts, and inconsistent income patterns can create confusion and raise red flags. Borrowers must ensure that their bank statements reflect a clear and consistent flow of income. This often requires planning months in advance, maintaining organized accounts, and avoiding unnecessary financial activity that could complicate the underwriting process.

Another critical mistake is failing to understand how income is calculated. Many borrowers assume that all deposits will be counted as income, but this is not the case. Lenders exclude non-recurring deposits, such as transfers, loans, or one-time payments. Additionally, business accounts are subject to expense factors, which can significantly reduce qualifying income. Without a clear understanding of these calculations, borrowers may overestimate their borrowing capacity and encounter issues during underwriting.

Credit mismanagement is another common pitfall. While jumbo bank statement loans offer flexibility in income documentation, they often require stronger credit profiles to offset risk. High credit utilization, recent late payments, or new debt can negatively impact approval. Borrowers should focus on maintaining low utilization, making timely payments, and avoiding new credit inquiries before applying. Even small improvements in credit can have a significant impact on loan terms and approval chances.

Timing mistakes can also be costly. Applying for a loan during a period of financial instability—such as fluctuating income, recent large transactions, or incomplete documentation—can lead to challenges. Borrowers should carefully plan their application timing, ensuring that their financial profile is stable and well-prepared. This includes having consistent deposits, sufficient reserves, and optimized credit.

Another common issue is insufficient reserves. Jumbo loans require a strong financial cushion, and failing to meet reserve requirements can result in denial. Borrowers must ensure that they have enough liquid assets to cover the required number of months of housing payments. This often involves strategic planning, such as consolidating funds or delaying certain investments to meet lender expectations.

Loan-to-value miscalculations are another frequent mistake. Borrowers may aim for the maximum allowable LTV without considering how it impacts their overall profile. Higher LTVs increase risk and may require stronger compensating factors. In many cases, increasing the down payment slightly can significantly improve approval chances and loan terms. Understanding how LTV interacts with other factors is essential.

Debt-to-income ratio is another area where mistakes occur. Borrowers may overlook existing obligations or fail to account for how income is calculated, leading to higher-than-expected DTIs. Managing debt strategically, paying down balances, and accurately calculating obligations can prevent issues during underwriting.

Another critical mistake is poor documentation. Jumbo loans require detailed and accurate documentation, and missing or incomplete information can delay the process. Borrowers should ensure that all documents are organized, up to date, and clearly presented. This includes bank statements, asset statements, and any additional documentation required to verify income and financial activity.

Communication breakdowns can also create challenges. Failing to respond promptly to lender requests or providing incomplete information can slow down the process and create frustration. Maintaining clear and consistent communication with your lender is essential for a smooth transaction.

Property-related issues are another potential obstacle. High-value properties must meet appraisal and marketability standards. Choosing a property that aligns with lender expectations can simplify the process and reduce the likelihood of complications. Understanding how property characteristics impact approval is an important part of the strategy.

Another common mistake is making financial changes during the loan process. Taking on new debt, making large purchases, or changing income sources can impact your approval. Lenders expect stability from application to closing, and any changes can trigger additional review. Maintaining consistency is critical.

Overconfidence can also be a risk. Some borrowers assume that strong income or assets alone will guarantee approval. However, jumbo lending is about balance. A strong profile in one area does not automatically compensate for weaknesses in others. Understanding the importance of a well-rounded financial profile is key.

Another important consideration is lender selection. Not all lenders have the same guidelines or risk tolerance. Choosing the wrong lender can lead to unnecessary challenges or denial. Working with knowledgeable professionals who understand the jumbo landscape can help you find the right fit.

Preparation is the most effective way to avoid mistakes. By reviewing your financial profile, identifying potential issues, and addressing them in advance, you can significantly improve your chances of success. This includes optimizing credit, building reserves, and structuring income appropriately.

Another key strategy is scenario planning. Evaluating different loan scenarios—such as varying down payments or income structures—can help you identify the most favorable approach.

This proactive planning allows you to make informed decisions and avoid surprises. Ultimately, avoiding mistakes in jumbo bank statement lending is about awareness, preparation, and execution. By understanding the common pitfalls and taking steps to mitigate them, you can position yourself for a successful and efficient loan process.

Real-Life Math Example: Avoiding Mistakes and Strengthening Approval

Consider a borrower named Rachel, a self-employed consultant looking to purchase a property priced at $1,750,000. Rachel initially believes she is well-qualified, but several issues arise during the loan process.

Rachel provides twelve months of bank statements showing total deposits of $1,050,000, resulting in an average monthly income of $87,500. The lender applies a 50% expense factor, reducing her qualifying income to $43,750 per month.

Her estimated monthly housing payment is $13,500, and she has $4,500 in additional monthly debt, bringing her total obligations to $18,000. Dividing $18,000 by $43,750 results in a DTI of approximately 41.1%, which is at the upper limit for many jumbo programs.

Rachel plans to put down 20%, resulting in an LTV of 80%. However, her lender requires a lower LTV due to her higher

DTI and credit score of 680. Additionally, her reserves are only $80,000, which equates to less than six months of reserves—below the lender's requirement.

Rachel also has several large deposits in her bank statements that are not clearly documented, leading to additional conditions during underwriting.

To address these issues, Rachel takes several steps. First, she works with her CPA to provide a profit and loss statement showing a lower expense ratio of 35%, increasing her qualifying income to approximately $56,875 per month. This reduces her DTI to 31.6%.

Next, Rachel increases her down payment to 25%, lowering her LTV to 75% and reducing the lender's risk. She also transfers additional funds into liquid accounts, increasing her reserves to $180,000, or over thirteen months.

Rachel pays down credit card balances, improving her credit score to 710, and provides documentation for the large deposits, clarifying their sources.

With these adjustments, Rachel's profile becomes significantly stronger. Her lower DTI, improved credit, increased reserves, and reduced LTV create a balanced and low-risk profile.

The lender reviews her updated application and approves the loan. Rachel successfully purchases the property, having overcome initial challenges through strategic adjustments.

This example demonstrates how common mistakes can impact a loan application and how they can be addressed. By understanding the factors that influence approval and taking proactive steps, borrowers can transform potential obstacles into opportunities for success.

It highlights the importance of preparation, attention to detail, and strategic planning. With the right approach, even complex jumbo loan scenarios can be navigated successfully.

Chapter 15

Becoming a Jumbo Bank Statement Loan Expert and Creating Long-Term Financial Freedom

As you arrive at the final chapter of this series, the focus shifts from learning and application to mastery and identity. At this level, you are no longer simply a borrower navigating the system—you are someone who understands how the system works, how to position yourself within it, and how to use it as a tool to create long-term financial freedom. Becoming a jumbo bank statement loan expert is not about memorizing guidelines; it is about developing a mindset, a strategy, and a repeatable approach that allows you to consistently achieve your financial goals.

The journey to mastery begins with perspective. Throughout this series, you have learned that jumbo bank statement loans are not just financing tools—they are strategic instruments. They allow you to leverage your true income, access high-value assets, and create opportunities that extend far beyond traditional lending limitations. When you understand this, you begin to see each loan not as an isolated transaction, but as part of a larger financial system that you control. One of the defining characteristics of experts in this space is intentionality. Every decision is made with purpose. From how income is structured to how assets are allocated, each element is aligned with a broader strategy. This level of control allows you to optimize outcomes, minimize risk, and create a financial profile that consistently meets lender expectations. Intentionality transforms reactive decisions into proactive strategies.

Another key aspect of mastery is adaptability. The lending landscape is constantly evolving, influenced by market conditions, interest rates, and investor appetite. Experts understand that flexibility is essential. They stay informed, adjust their strategies as needed, and take advantage of opportunities as they arise. This ability to adapt ensures that they remain competitive and effective, regardless of external changes.

Financial discipline is the backbone of long-term success. Maintaining consistent income, managing debt responsibly, and building reserves are not one-time actions—they are ongoing habits. Experts understand that their financial behavior directly impacts their ability to access future opportunities. By maintaining discipline, they create a stable foundation that supports continuous growth. Another important element is scalability. True mastery involves building a system that can grow over time. This means structuring your finances in a way that supports multiple transactions, maintaining strong reserves, and avoiding over-leverage. A scalable system allows you to expand your portfolio, increase your income, and create compounding returns without compromising stability.

Leverage, when used correctly, becomes a powerful tool for wealth creation. Jumbo bank statement loans allow you to control high-value assets with a relatively smaller amount of capital. Experts understand how to use this leverage strategically, balancing risk and reward. They know when to increase leverage to accelerate growth and when to reduce it to preserve stability.

Another defining trait of experts is their ability to think in terms of systems rather than transactions. Each loan, property, and financial decision is part of a larger framework. This framework includes acquisition, optimization, and exit strategies. By viewing their financial journey as a system, experts are able to make decisions that align with long-term goals rather than short-term gains.

Education and continuous learning are also critical. The most successful individuals in this space are those who remain curious and committed to improving their knowledge. They study market trends, analyze new lending programs, and refine their strategies over time. This commitment to growth ensures that they remain ahead of the curve and capable of navigating complex scenarios.

Another important aspect is risk awareness. Experts do not avoid risk—they manage it. They understand that every opportunity comes with potential challenges, and they take steps to mitigate those risks. This includes maintaining reserves, diversifying their portfolio, and avoiding overexposure to any single asset or market. By managing risk effectively, they protect their financial foundation while pursuing growth.

Networking and relationships play a significant role in mastery. Building connections with lenders, brokers, and financial professionals provides access to valuable insights and opportunities. These relationships can help you navigate challenges, identify favorable programs, and streamline the loan process. Over time, a strong network becomes a key asset in your financial journey.

Another critical component is clarity of goals. Experts have a clear vision of what they want to achieve, whether it is financial independence, portfolio growth, or lifestyle enhancement. This clarity guides their decisions and ensures that each step aligns with their objectives. Without clear goals, it becomes difficult to measure progress or make informed decisions.

Mindset is perhaps the most important factor of all. Success in jumbo bank statement lending requires confidence, patience, and resilience. There will be challenges, setbacks, and moments of uncertainty. Experts understand that these are part of the process and remain focused on their long-term vision. They approach each situation with a problem-solving mindset, finding solutions rather than dwelling on obstacles.

Another advanced concept is optimization. This involves continuously refining your financial profile to achieve better outcomes. This may include improving credit, increasing reserves, restructuring income, or adjusting your portfolio. Optimization is an ongoing process that ensures your financial system remains efficient and effective.

As you reflect on everything you have learned, it becomes clear that becoming a jumbo bank statement loan expert is not a destination—it is a journey. It is about applying knowledge, refining strategies, and continuously improving. Each transaction, each decision, and each experience contributes to your growth and success.

Ultimately, the goal is financial freedom. This means having the ability to make choices based on your goals and values rather than financial constraints. Jumbo bank statement loans provide a pathway to this freedom by allowing you to leverage your income, access high-value assets, and create long-term wealth.

By mastering the principles outlined in this series, you have the tools to take control of your financial future. You can navigate complex lending scenarios, build a scalable system, and create opportunities that align with your vision. The journey does not end here—it evolves as you continue to grow, learn, and succeed.

Real-Life Math Example: Achieving Financial Freedom Through Strategic Jumbo Lending

Consider a borrower named Adrian, a self-employed entrepreneur who has spent the past decade building a portfolio of high-value properties using jumbo bank statement loans. Adrian's goal is to achieve financial freedom by creating a system that generates consistent income while preserving long-term wealth.

Adrian's current portfolio consists of four properties valued at $1,500,000, $1,800,000, $2,200,000, and $2,500,000, for a total value of $8,000,000. His combined loan balances total $4,200,000, leaving him with $3,800,000 in equity.

Adrian's annual deposits total $1,800,000, resulting in an average monthly income of $150,000. Applying a 40% expense factor, his qualifying income is $90,000 per month. His total monthly mortgage payments across all properties are $30,000, resulting in a DTI of 33.3%.

Adrian decides to optimize his portfolio. He performs a cash-out refinance on his $2,500,000 property. At a 70% LTV, he can borrow $1,750,000. With an existing loan balance of $1,200,000, he accesses $550,000 in cash.

He uses this cash to pay down $200,000 in debt across his other properties, reducing his monthly obligations by $3,000. He also invests $350,000 into a new property priced at $1,400,000, putting down 25% and securing a loan for the remaining balance.

Adrian's income continues to grow, with annual deposits increasing to $2,100,000, resulting in a monthly income of $175,000. After applying a 40% expense factor, his qualifying income is $105,000 per month.

His updated monthly obligations total $35,000. Dividing $35,000 by $105,000 results in a DTI of 33.3%, maintaining a stable ratio despite portfolio growth.

Adrian also increases his rental income through property improvements and better management, raising his monthly income from $25,000 to $35,000. This additional cash flow enhances his financial stability and provides a buffer for future investments.

Over time, Adrian continues to refine his strategy, balancing leverage, cash flow, and equity. He gradually reduces debt while maintaining strong income, creating a system that generates consistent returns.

Eventually, Adrian reaches a point where his rental income covers all his expenses, allowing him to achieve financial freedom. His portfolio continues to appreciate, and his equity grows, providing long-term wealth and security.

This example demonstrates how mastering jumbo bank statement lending can lead to financial independence. By applying strategic thinking, disciplined management, and continuous optimization, Adrian transforms his financial profile into a powerful system for wealth creation.

It highlights the importance of viewing each transaction as part of a larger strategy. With the right approach, borrowers can move beyond individual loans and create a sustainable path to long-term success and freedom.

Final Thoughts

As you reach the end of this journey through the Bank Statement Mortgage Loan Mastery Series, it is important to pause and reflect on what you have truly gained. This is more than just knowledge about mortgage products, underwriting guidelines, or financial calculations. What you now possess is a framework—a way of thinking, analyzing, and positioning yourself in a financial system that most people never fully understand. You have learned how to see beyond traditional limitations, how to recognize opportunity where others see barriers, and how to take control of your financial narrative in a way that aligns with your goals.

Throughout this series, one theme has remained constant: you are not defined by how your income appears on paper. Traditional lending systems were built around a narrow definition of income—one that often excludes entrepreneurs, self-employed individuals, and those who operate outside of conventional employment structures. Bank statement mortgage loans challenge that definition. They recognize that real income is not always captured in tax returns, and they provide a pathway for individuals to leverage their true earning potential. This shift in perspective is powerful, because it allows you to move from being constrained by the system to actively navigating it. At the jumbo level, this understanding becomes even more valuable. High-value properties, larger loan amounts, and more complex financial profiles require a deeper level of strategy and preparation. You have learned that success in this space is not about meeting minimum requirements—it is about building a complete, well-balanced financial profile. It is about understanding how income, credit, reserves, loan-to-value, and property characteristics interact to form a cohesive story that lenders can trust.

One of the most important lessons you should take away is the concept of control. You have more control over your financial profile than you may have realized before. You can influence how your income is presented, how your credit is managed, how your reserves are structured, and how your overall profile is perceived. This control allows you to shift from a reactive mindset—where you hope to qualify—to a proactive mindset—where you position yourself for approval.

Another key takeaway is the importance of preparation. Success in jumbo bank statement lending is rarely accidental. It is the result of deliberate planning, disciplined financial behavior, and strategic decision-making. Preparing months in advance, maintaining consistent deposits, optimizing credit, and building reserves are all actions that contribute to a stronger application. When you approach the process with preparation, you reduce uncertainty and increase your chances of success.

As you move forward, it is essential to think in terms of systems rather than transactions. Each loan, each property, and each financial decision should be part of a larger strategy. Whether your goal is to purchase a primary residence, build an investment portfolio, or achieve financial independence, your actions should align with that vision. By thinking in systems, you create a framework that allows you to scale, adapt, and grow over time.

Another critical concept is balance. Jumbo bank statement loans offer flexibility, but they also require responsibility. Balancing leverage with stability, growth with risk management, and investment with liquidity is essential. Overextending can create challenges, while underutilizing opportunities can limit growth. Finding the right balance ensures that your financial strategy remains sustainable and effective.

You have also learned the importance of adaptability. The financial landscape is constantly changing, influenced by market conditions, interest rates, and lending guidelines. Staying informed and being willing to adjust your strategy is key to long-term success. Adaptability allows you to navigate challenges, take advantage of opportunities, and remain resilient in the face of uncertainty. Another powerful lesson is the role of mindset. Your approach to this process will often determine your outcome. Confidence, patience, and persistence are essential qualities. There may be obstacles, delays, or unexpected challenges along the way, but these are part of the journey. By maintaining a problem-solving mindset and focusing on solutions, you can overcome these challenges and continue moving forward.

Financial discipline remains at the core of everything you do. Consistent income management, responsible credit behavior, and maintaining reserves are not one-time actions—they are ongoing habits. These habits form the foundation of your financial profile and influence every opportunity you pursue. Discipline creates stability, and stability creates opportunity.

Another important aspect is the ability to see opportunity where others do not. Many borrowers are discouraged by traditional lending limitations and assume that they cannot qualify for certain opportunities. You now understand that alternative solutions exist, and that with the right strategy, you can access opportunities that may seem out of reach. This perspective gives you a significant advantage.

As you think about your future, consider the role of long-term vision. Financial success is not built overnight—it is the result of consistent effort, strategic planning, and compounding growth over time. Each decision you make should contribute to your long-term goals, whether that involves building a portfolio, creating passive income, or achieving financial independence.

Another key element is the importance of relationships. Working with knowledgeable professionals, including lenders, brokers, and financial advisors, can provide valuable insights and support. These relationships can help you navigate complex scenarios, identify opportunities, and streamline the process. Building a strong network is an investment in your success.

Risk management is also a critical component of long-term success. Every opportunity comes with potential challenges, and understanding how to manage risk is essential. This includes maintaining reserves, diversifying your portfolio, and avoiding over-leverage. By managing risk effectively, you protect your financial foundation while pursuing growth.

As you continue to apply what you have learned, remember that growth is a continuous process. Each experience, each transaction, and each decision provides an opportunity to learn and improve. By staying committed to your goals and refining your strategy, you can continue to build on your success.

Ultimately, this series is about empowerment. It is about giving you the knowledge, tools, and confidence to take control of your financial future. Jumbo bank statement mortgage loans are not just a means to an end—they are a gateway to opportunity, growth, and long-term wealth.

The journey does not end here. In many ways, it is just beginning. You now have the foundation to move forward with clarity and confidence. Whether you are purchasing your first high-value property or expanding an existing portfolio, you have the ability to navigate the process with precision and purpose.

As you take your next steps, remember that success is not defined by a single transaction—it is defined by the system you build and the consistency with which you execute it. Stay focused, stay disciplined, and continue to refine your approach. The opportunities are there, and with the knowledge you now possess, you are fully equipped to seize them.

Your financial future is no longer something that happens to you—it is something you create.

How to Get a Personalized Bank Statement Mortgage Review

If you found this book helpful, you may want to see how these strategies apply to your specific financial situation.

Bank statement mortgage lending is highly customized—your deposits, income patterns, expense ratios, credit profile, property type, and long-term goals all play a role in determining what you qualify for and how your loan should be structured.

Every borrower's situation is different. The way your income flows through your accounts, how your business operates, your credit history, the property you are purchasing or refinancing, and current lender guidelines all impact your options. The strategies and examples in this book are designed to teach you how bank statement mortgage loans work—but your actual qualifying income, loan amount, and loan structure can only be determined by analyzing your real financial profile.

If you would like a no-obligation Bank Statement Mortgage review, you can request one here:

Email: info@FinibiMortgage.com

A licensed mortgage broker will review your bank statements, income structure, credit profile, and goals, and explain what bank statement mortgage options may be available to you—including:

• 12-month and 24-month bank statement programs• Personal vs business bank statement qualification• Primary residence and investment property financing• Cash-out refinance and equity access strategies• Advanced structuring to maximize qualifying income

No cost. No pressure. No obligation.

Sincerely,

Joseph G. Correa

Finibi Mortgage Inc.

Licensed Mortgage Broker

About the Author

Joseph G. Correa is a licensed mortgage broker and the founder of Finibi Mortgage, a Florida-based brokerage specializing in bank statement mortgage loans, non-QM lending, and strategic real estate financing solutions for self-employed borrowers, entrepreneurs, and investors.

With more than two decades of experience in mortgage lending, underwriting, and deal structuring, Joseph has helped thousands of clients qualify for real estate using alternative income documentation, unlocking opportunities that traditional lending often restricts.

Unlike traditional loan officers who rely strictly on tax returns and W-2 income, Joseph's approach focuses on real cash flow, income structuring, and financial strategy. He believes that borrowers should not be limited by how income is reported on paper, but instead empowered by how income is actually earned and managed.

Joseph is widely recognized for his expertise in:

• Bank statement mortgage loans• Self-employed borrower financing• Non-QM and alternative income lending• Investment property and portfolio financing• Cash-out refinance and equity strategies• Advanced mortgage loan structuring

Through his education platform, Finibi Academy, Joseph has trained tens of thousands of students worldwide in mortgage strategy, real estate investing, credit optimization, and financial independence.

He created the **Bank Statement Mortgage Loan Mastery Series** to provide a clear, step-by-step roadmap for borrowers and professionals who want to qualify for real estate without relying on traditional income documentation.

His mission is simple: To help people use their real income—not just their tax returns—to qualify, invest, and build long-term wealth.

When he is not structuring loans or writing, Joseph works with clients across the United States to design customized mortgage strategies that align with their financial goals, income structure, and long-term investment plans.

The Bank Statement Mortgage Loan Mastery Series Roadmap

The Complete Guide to Qualifying for Real Estate Using Bank Statements Instead of Tax Returns

The purpose of the **Bank Statement Mortgage Loan Mastery Series** is to give borrowers, investors, and mortgage professionals the exact strategies used by lenders and underwriters—translated into simple, practical steps you can apply in real life.

This series takes you from beginner to advanced mastery of how to qualify, structure, and scale real estate financing using bank statements instead of traditional income.

Each book builds on the last. You are not just learning how to get approved—you are learning how to control your approvals.

Book 1 — Bank Statement Mortgage Loan Fundamentals

Learn how bank statement loans work, how income is calculated, and why tax returns are no longer required for many borrowers.

Book 2 — Personal Bank Statement Mortgage Loans

Learn how to qualify using personal accounts, structure

deposits, and maximize usable income.

Book 3 — Business Bank Statement Mortgage Loans

Understand how lenders analyze business revenue, apply expense ratios, and use P&Ls.

Book 4 — Bank Statement Loans for Self-Employed Borrowers

Master how entrepreneurs qualify and structure income for approval.

Book 5 — Bank Statement Loans for Primary Residences

Learn how to buy or refinance your home using bank statement income.

Book 6 — Bank Statement Loans for Investment Properties

Discover how to scale rental portfolios using bank statement + DSCR strategies.

Book 7 — Jumbo Bank Statement Mortgage Loans

Learn how to finance high-value properties with advanced requirements and structuring.

Book 8 — Bank Statement Loan Refinancing & Cash-Out Strategies

Unlock equity, reduce payments, and reinvest capital using bank statement refinancing.

Book 9 — Bank Statement Loans with Credit Challenges

Learn how to qualify even with lower credit using compensating factors and strategy.

Book 10 — Advanced Bank Statement Mortgage Loan Structuring

Engineer approvals using deposits, expense ratios, and lender guidelines.

This series is designed to move you from understanding → execution → mastery.

By the end, you will not just know how to qualify—you will know how to structure deals like a professional.

Educational & Financial Disclaimer

The **Bank Statement Mortgage Loan Mastery Series** is intended for educational and informational purposes only.

This content is designed to help readers understand bank statement mortgage lending, real estate financing strategies, and income structuring concepts. It is not financial, legal, tax, or investment advice.

Joseph G. Correa and Live Stronger Faster are not acting as your personal financial advisor, attorney, accountant, or mortgage professional through this publication.

Mortgage guidelines, underwriting standards, interest rates, and loan programs vary by lender and may change at any time without notice.

All examples in this series are for illustration purposes only and do not guarantee approval or results.

Always consult with licensed professionals before making financial decisions.

Risk Disclosure

Bank statement mortgage lending and real estate investing involve risk.

Income fluctuations, interest rate changes, market conditions, and lender guidelines can all impact loan approval and financial outcomes.

Borrowing against real estate or using leverage increases both potential returns and risks.

Failure to repay a loan may result in foreclosure and loss of property.

Cash flow, rental income, and appreciation are not guaranteed.

All strategies in this series are educational and must be evaluated based on your individual financial situation.

You are solely responsible for your financial decisions.